ROLE OF A
LIFETIME

ROLE OF A LIFETIME

Reflections on Faith,
Family, and
Significant Living

James Brown

with Nathan Whitaker

Foreword by Tony Dungy

New York Boston Nashville

FaithWords
Hachette Book Group
237 Park Avenue
New York, NY 10017

Visit our website at www.faithwords.com.

Printed in the United States of America

First Edition: September 2009

10   9   8   7   6   5   4   3   2   1

FaithWords is a division of Hachette Book Group, Inc.
The FaithWords name and logo are trademarks of
Hachette Book Group, Inc.

Library of Congress Cataloging-in-Publication Data

Brown, James, 1951 Feb. 25–
   Role of a lifetime : reflections on faith, family, and significant
living / James Brown, with Nathan Whitaker. — 1st ed.
      p. cm.
   ISBN 978-0-446-54117-6
   1. Brown, James, 1951 Feb. 25–   2. Sportscasters—United
States—Biography.   3. Inspiration.   I. Title.
   GV742.42.B77A3 2009
   796.092—dc22
   [B]

                                                2009012147

*This book is dedicated to my parents, John and
Mary Ann Brown. I thank GOD for the lifetime roles
they performed in raising their children.*

*They were steadfast in their commitment to family, tireless
in their efforts to provide a better life, passionate in instilling
in us a spirit of excellence, and modeled an unwavering
belief that doing things GOD's way is ALWAYS the right way.
I'm extremely grateful.*

CONTENTS

FOREWORD

James Brown is an uncommon personality in sports broadcasting today. He has become one of the most recognizable faces, and voices, in the industry. He not only hosts CBS's National Football League pre-game show but has appeared on national television broadcasts of college and professional sports, as well as the Olympics. His voice is heard on daily and weekly radio broadcasts. While he is now recognized as one of the best in his field, the journey hasn't always been smooth. In *Role of a Lifetime* James not only shares the details of this journey, but also the life lessons that were learned from some great mentors he's had along the way.

I first met the man everyone calls "JB" in the late 1980s (JB may remember the exact year) when I was an assistant coach for the Pittsburgh Steelers and he was doing play-by-play for CBS. He would always come in early and ask questions about our players to prepare for the broadcasts. What I noticed right away was that he not only wanted to know their assignments on the field, so he could report accurately on the game, but he also wanted to know about them as men. He always wanted to highlight what they were doing off the field that the viewers may not know about. As I got to know him better, I learned that this is what James Brown is all about—not football or basketball, but about people and relationships.

That's what makes James so unique in his business. To get to the top in broadcasting you usually have to put the spotlight on yourself and demonstrate how good *you* are and how much *you* know. But James has taken a different approach, taking the advice of his high school coach and choosing to be a "role player"—a player who does the little things to help his teammates to look better. By using this game plan and by following Christ's model of servant leadership he has become not only one of the best, but also one of the most respected and well-liked broadcasters of our time.

In this book you'll see how that life philosophy was developed, starting with the work ethic that was instilled in him by his parents while growing up in Washington, DC. You will see a commitment to preparation and teamwork that grew through basketball at DeMatha High School and Harvard University, and was later fine-tuned by a stint in the business world. You'll see a professional career of groundbreaking achievements mixed with setbacks and disappointments. And ultimately, you'll discover what has allowed him to gracefully handle everything that has come his way—his faith in Jesus Christ.

That faith is what makes James Brown special. Not only did his faith allow him to move forward in those tough times, it's what has allowed him to remain humble in a business characterized by huge egos. It's what has motivated him to utilize the platform and visibility of national television, not for personal gain, but to help others. It's that faith in God that guides him daily and shapes every decision he makes.

James Brown has been a great friend and role model for me and so many others in the sports world over the years. Now, by writing this book, I believe he will inspire even more people who get to know the story behind this uncommon man.

—Tony Dungy

ACKNOWLEDGMENTS

I did my best to think of the most effective, inclusive way of thanking all of the people who have been so helpful to me. It proved to be THE most difficult task. Even if I were to have devoted a chapter in the book for acknowledgments, I would think of someone, after the fact, whose name I forgot. That would hurt me more than the person not mentioned. So, please forgive me for not taking the risk.

Therefore, for each and every person who has played a meaningful role in shaping the person I am today—and you know who you are—I am DEEPLY grateful.

I think everyone would understand my singling out my family. My wife Dorothy, who means as much to me as the air I breathe, is a blessing beyond measure, and the catalyst for my spiritual growth. My brothers, John, Terence and Everett and my Uncle Cliff who not only have been ardent supporters, but friends who provide me with candid, helpful feedback. My sister, Alicia is not only the smartest one in the family, but the one to whom we owe a debt of gratitude. She shared a home with mom and was her principal caretaker thru Mom's long battle with health challenges, all the while managing responsibilities as a big company vice president. There's nothing like the love of a daughter, and Katrina is my pride and joy. She and my son-in-law John, have given me another reason to continue working hard and set the right example in my granddaughter, Kaela.

Acknowledgments

My two adopted family members include my high school coach, confident and trusted family friend Morgan Wootten; and the person who not only convinced me, but got me excited about writing this book, my attorney Jeff Fried.

I especially want to thank my friends at FaithWords who were as patient as anyone could expect, given the demands on my time during the NFL season, especially Rolf Zettersten, Harry Helm, and Gina Wynn. I'm sure working with me has given them a new appreciation for the words, long-suffering.

I'd like to thank my colleagues at CBS, both my studio co-hosts and particularly all of those great people behind-the-scenes. You never get to see them but without them, the shot itself would not be as good as it is. They are family and I love them.

Thanks to my Literary Agent Jake Elwell who helped me to find the right home for this book. And to my co-author Nathan Whitaker. He's a bright, quick-witted, humble man with whom I've become good friends. My assistant Elizabeth Malia continues to amaze me with the many hats she wears so well.

To Tony Dungy, who encouraged me to be as open and as bold as possible in writing this book. That performing my role in this lifetime will continue to be a success by esteeming others above myself.

Finally, but most importantly, to My LORD and SAVIOR, JESUS CHRIST. To GOD be the glory. In all that I do, I seek to do excellently unto HIM.

INTRODUCTION

> But seek ye first the kingdom of God,
> and his righteousness; and all these
> things shall be added unto you.
>
> *Matthew 6:33* (KJV)

We may not have met yet, but I suspect that we have a lot in common, you and I.

For whatever reason that brought you to pick up this book, I am grateful that you did, and for the time and attention you will give to the pages that follow. In some ways, I'm not sure my story is any different from that of the typical twenty-first century American out there—a tale of searching through life to find who I was, who I was created to be, and what I was meant to do. It is a journey of perseverance to overcome obstacles and make it to the end of valleys that far too often we find in front of us.

I suspect your journey has been a lot like mine.

At the same time, I do recognize that I also have lived a real-life fairy tale of finding myself in the loving embrace of a woman, a family, and a Savior who loves me for who I am, flaws and all. I have been blessed beyond measure with experiences and opportunities that are far beyond what I had envisioned or have merited, and I have tried to stop long enough to savor those at every twist and turn along the way.

And so, when I was told over the years that I had something to write about by a variety of people, I initially reacted with hesitation. I dismissed out of hand their contention that I really had anything to offer that was either unique or of interest, and pushed the thought aside, to the deeper recesses of my mind. As you can see, I apparently didn't completely cast it aside, because their encouraging words began to slowly come back into my conscious thoughts.

In the meantime, though, my good friend Indianapolis Colts coach Tony Dungy came out with his memoir, and a radio personality and I were talking about the book. It seems that this radio personality, who has a wildly popular talk show because of his antagonistic, "shock-jock" type format, had read Tony's book and was so moved by it that he began reconsidering his life's work. "JB, I realized after reading that book that I don't want to look back and think that this is what I did with the talents I've got—to inflame and upset people. That can't be my legacy."

That conversation led me to talk with Tony about the encouragement I had received to write about my journey, and realized, like Coach Dungy's motivation to finally share his life's story in *Quiet Strength*, that if there was even one person who drew something out of my book that positively impacted them and how they navigated the journey of their own life, that would make it worth the effort. Conversations with my friend and attorney Jeff Fried brought to the forefront many of the pearls of wisdom, heart-to-heart discussions, and flat-out orders from my mother—which ultimately laid the foundation upon which I've lived. *Her* example was the best. Realizing that, I wanted to honor my mother's and my father's legacies. My dad was more like the biblical character Joseph: the strong, supportive, caring, silent type who ably provided for us. Two devoted, sacrificing parents with only high school educations, but PhD's in common sense and love.

And so, with that perspective, I reflected further on the incredible experiences I have enjoyed, the disappointments I have endured, those saints along the way who built themselves into my life, and upon the faith that has carried me through it all.

There are things that I have learned, there are giants in my life that have lifted me up that I might see and go farther, and there are stories that might lighten your day. Yes, there are things that I can share. Things that may help you and others. Things that may give you strength for your journey. Things that just may bring a different perspective to whatever you may be facing. But recognize that I do so with gratitude toward you in deciding to come along with me on my journey. I haven't always gotten it right, but if sharing from some of the times when I've gotten it wrong will help you, I will be humbled by that experience.

Role of a Lifetime is premised on the belief that *finding and playing the role we were meant to play* should be our goal. It's a place where we find not only success, but real significance in each day. On that journey, allowing others to shine, and helping them to do so in *their* roles, can be the best way to live out this life we've been given and to maximize its impact and find fulfillment along the way.

This book is designed to be more than simply a memoir. While the stories of my life may provide moments of enjoyment, I hope that even more they will illuminate the life lessons learned along my journey—the satisfaction I have enjoyed by focusing on and embracing my own gifts and abilities, and striving to make the most of the roles that have come my way that I have chosen to play.

All generations are searching for answers and looking for them in the lives of high-profile examples—whom society lifts as role models—who too often live by relative values and are themselves looking for guidance. You and I live in a world that all too often operates under the overriding template of self-promotion, embracing a "Hooray for Me" attitude, and which measures success in increasingly small time snapshots dotted with markers of temporal value. From a lifetime of experiences—both good and not so good—I have learned that a life of real significance will not be found by following that path.

In addition, society preaches that if you follow the latest formula for success, you can be the *best*. The reality, however, is that not all of us will end up on the top rung of the ladder—wherever that is. And even if we do, we will feel unfulfilled when we get there (maybe even along the way), ultimately realizing that is not where we were meant to be.

Instead, my goal has been to do the right thing the right way, all of the time, and through that to make the most of my role—whatever it may be. We may not all be called to be the leader in the journey—instead, many of us are called to play a different role. And if we pause to consider it, we realize we all have roles that are unique to us and shaped by our gifts and abilities. All sorts of meaningful life-changing roles. Son. Daughter. Wife. Husband. Father. Mother. Friend. Co-worker. Coach. Employer. Teacher. Roles that make the world a better place and that impact lives for good.

I wasn't born with all the answers—far from it—but have learned through the journey of my life, from the influential people who guided me, and from the events, both personal and societal, which challenged, scarred, at times, and shaped me, that life is about the longer view. I still don't have all the answers, but have learned that success in life—overcoming the difficulties and detours—is really about the deeper meaning in everything you do, the significant difference you make while striving to honor God and leaving a legacy of changed lives. In that, I have found the blessings of a life of satisfaction, impact, joy, and fulfillment.

My hope and prayer is that this book will help you to see a bit of what I have seen through my journey, that it will bless you in some way, and that you will find something to take from it—some encouragement, some measure of wisdom, or a dose of inspiration, for successful and more significant living. Maybe you will take away something as simple as this thought, which will surely overcome you at times as you read: "I'll never make the mistake JB made in that situation!" Maybe you will begin to see that who you have been created to be is something of incredible and of eternal value, and the roles that you occupy in life, no one else can occupy.

This book is experiential in nature, in that I'm not much of a historian. I don't always remember dates or the exact sequence of events, but I am not afraid to show emotion—yes, even shed a tear or two—and can remember exactly how I *felt* when something meaningful occurred. The book, therefore, will wend its way from meaningful event to meaningful event—as I saw them—as I recollect my story.

And so, this is simply my story, humbly offered: those things that have worked—and all those that haven't!—for me so far, and the people that have helped get me here, and the experiences that have shaped me in the journey. Along the way, there will be some laughs, many laughs, since I have had the privilege of working with some crazy people, whom I love dearly.

Through it all, my journey is now inseparably entwined with my Savior who has been with me throughout—even at times when I wasn't sure—and continues to this day to walk beside me and provide me with strength, courage, and wisdom far beyond my own capabilities. He has always smiled down upon me—even when I may not have deserved it—as I did my best to find and fill the roles He put before me.

I suspect, as you come along beside me, we may find that we have a lot in common, you and I.

ROLE OF A
LIFETIME

ONE SAVANNAH SUMMER

You're either progressing as a player or regressing.

Morgan Wootten

This was not how it was supposed to be. The noise from the landing gear grinding into place pierced the fog of my thoughts. The blanket of clouds outside the window of our plane stretched as far as I could see and was thick, hiding my next stop. In a few minutes we would break through them and touch down—then what?

How would I explain it to my family, and all my friends? What would I say to all those people who watched, supported, and cheered me on for so long? What would I say to all the kids in the neighborhood who had looked up to me for all those years? How could I look at myself in the mirror?

My teammates. Coach Harrison. The Washingtons, Smiths, Kellys, Winslows, and others in the neighborhood. My girlfriend.

And Coach Wootten. What would he say? Every step and stop along the way of my basketball career had been up. Oh, there had been some setbacks, some roadblocks, some learning moments—always the temporary hinderances of hard work, and always followed by more success. More wins. More people who noticed my athletic ability and progress. My potential to play on a bigger stage was becoming clear. Basketball would be my ticket to a successful, fulfilling, and meaningful life.

No more. What in the world was next?

I knew that this was where I belonged. This was where I was meant to be.

There were still six of us out on the basketball court. It had been a long workout and our bodies—white and black— were glistening and dripping with sweat. It had been a long training camp, but with the exhibition season fast approaching, we were getting in some extra work.

I was receiving an education in Savannah summers. They are incredibly hot, with little breeze, and even extended past what I had always considered to be a normal summer. DC certainly gets hot, but the grip of the summer heat at least starts to break a bit by September. Not only was it sweltering and still outside in the ninety-two degree Georgia heat, it was even hotter inside the Savannah Civic Center.

There were only sixteen or seventeen of us left in camp, and a handful of us were getting in some extra work after practice. It was a combined camp, consisting of the Atlanta Hawks veteran players along with a few of us rookies who had lasted this long.

This was both a culmination and a commencement. The apex of my basketball career to date, and yet merely the threshold of the true dream which God had placed in my heart, making use of the talents that He had given me. My professional basketball career lay before me: the dream of playing in the National Basketball Association with some of the best basketball players in the world. I felt I belonged. I was where I wanted to be. Shortly the twelve-man squad would be leaving the Savannah summer and its oppressive heat behind for the slightly cooler weather of an Atlanta autumn to begin the exhibition and regular season of 1973.

I had been drafted in the fourth round by the Atlanta Hawks of the NBA and in the sixth round by the Denver Rockets. The Rockets, of the American Basketball Association, opted to wait until the sixth round because they—correctly—had ascertained that I would prefer to play at the highest level, in the National Basketball Association. I had worked too hard and too diligently, and sacrificed too many other things for too many years to not pursue this at the highest level, with the Hawks, even if the Rockets were optimistic that I would make the squad. There were no such guarantees from the Hawks, but frankly, as I viewed the situation and my talents, I didn't need any. I was having a good camp, and like any competitive athlete, I had been taught that there was no challenge so great that I could not overcome it.

By all accounts, I was a leaper. I was hailed as one of the best leapers to come out of the District of Columbia basketball ranks, which helped offset my size—I am only six feet five inches tall. I would need every bit of that jumping ability if I was going to enjoy the long-lived career that I believed I would have in the NBA.

Some of the things taking place in that camp could be taught and learned. "Pistol" Pete Maravich was our star. He could do unbelievable things with a basketball—dribble between his legs and behind his back at full speed, and whip the craziest, unexpected passes your way, with mustard on them so you had to be alert or risk losing a tooth. He could dribble a basketball in each hand—two balls simultaneously—and beat me and the rest of the squad down the court, while each of us were only dribbling one ball.

Leaping ability, however, is something innate that inspires awe. Scouts looked for that, and other innate abilities that couldn't be taught. Those were the things that could make the difference between championships and mediocrity. That leaping ability had made me a high school center, even though I was relatively short by basketball standards. Humorously, I often tell people that I began high school as a six-foot, six-inch freshman, but graduated as a six-foot, five-inch senior. (It's conceivable that we may have "exaggerated" a bit in those early years.) As a center I had been a two-time high school All-American, and one of the top five prep players in the country, coming out of the storied basketball program at DeMatha Catholic High School in Washington, DC. In large part because of my leaping ability, that made me—by those who followed such things at the time—one of the greatest leapers in DC history.

Coming up I was tough playing inside—in the paint. I blocked shots and rebounded better than players far bigger than I was, employing a combination of what I would describe as ability and tenacity. My opponents might have characterized things a bit differently. But the truth is—I *wanted* the ball. I also had a very soft corner jump shot, which I could take out to the wing with similar success as well. I knew that in the NBA I couldn't be nearly as effective in the paint at six-five, so I was relying more and more on my outside game. My shooting touch had always been solid throughout high school and I worked to make it as reliable as possible when I was in college, and was moved from the center and forward positions I had played in high school to a small forward and big guard in college. But, to be honest, I had a *decent* outside shot.

The rest of my game hadn't developed as much in college as it probably should have, but I was a smooth, solid player and was establishing myself with an excellent camp as a number two guard, also called a shooting guard. I hadn't played a great deal in the backcourt, and still needed to polish up some of those areas of my game—ball control and ball handling, penetration, the transition game, more movement without the ball, and getting into the flow better on

5

the offensive side of the court. Still, it had gone well. So well that I was a three-time All–Ivy League selection.

And now, I had been selected by the Hawks in the 1973 NBA Draft. I was chosen after Dwight Jones of the University of Houston and John Brown of Missouri, their two first round picks, Tom Inglesby out of Villanova in the second round, and Ted Manakas of Princeton and Leonard Gray of Long Beach State were taken in the third round. There were twelve rounds then, and I was, I knew, competing with Ted and Leonard and the other players drafted behind me—except for Dave Winfield, taken in the fifth round, who they knew would go on to play baseball instead—for one spot on the twelve man roster. Counting the first three draft selections, the team stars Pete Maravich and Lou Hudson, and other returning veterans from the prior season's playoff team, I knew that Cotton Fitzsimmons, the head coach, and his staff had accounted for eleven spots. That was fine by me—that still left one spot. I just needed one spot.

I was going to be the twelfth.

⸙

We finally finished our extemporaneous pickup game of three-on-three, and I stayed to shoot a few more free throws. My effort hadn't been quite what it needed to be in college, even though I had done well, but I was making up for it during those first four weeks of camp. I had been steady, and felt that I would not only be able to hold up through an eighty-two game season but that, with hard and extra work, could improve even more rapidly and develop those other areas I would need to be able to contribute to the success of the team.

I finished my free throw time and decided to head down to the whirlpool in the Civic Center, to try to lessen the aches and pains that I would feel in my knees in the morning.

While I was in the whirlpool machine, treating my aching muscles, one of the assistants entered the trainer's room and found me. He told me that Coach Fitzsimmons wanted to meet with me. This wasn't unusual, by my way of thinking. Coach had been helpful all along to give me pointers on things to work on outside of practice, and now we were approaching the time to leave Savannah and head to Atlanta to start the slate of exhibition games. I showered and dressed quickly and headed up to his hotel room.

"JB, you've been a great guy, and it's been a pleasure to have had the chance to have you with us for the last few weeks." I nodded and smiled, but the smile melted from my lips as the realization of his use of the past tense began to sink in. My mind began racing, but I snapped out of it just in time to hear, "I'm going to let you go."

"You're kidding me," was all I could manage. It was unthinkable.

"You've got a great background, a great education, and I have no doubt that you will do great in the game of life," Coach Fitzsimmons said.

"Well, that's all well and fine, Coach. But I wasn't looking to do any of that right *now*. I want to play basketball right now in my life. This is what I'm good at. This is my future. Help me understand how I don't have what's necessary to make this team."

He didn't have a direct answer. He didn't have to—even though I thought I needed it at that moment. Whatever his answer—the deal was over. It was a matter of the numbers, he said. He simply needed to cut one more player, and I was that one.

I was devastated. Everything around me seemed out of place. It was surreal. There was no scenario I had imagined in which *this* was the possible outcome. Not one. I hadn't dreaded heading up to his hotel room, because it was always someone else being released. It certainly wasn't going to be me.

But this time it was me. The dream was over, already.

I couldn't imagine what was next. The thought that I wouldn't make the final roster had been unthinkable for me, when others were making alternative arrangements this summer. Now it was a reality. I hadn't prepared for, I hadn't even thought of a fallback plan for my life. College classmates were heading off to law school—no, they had already *begun* law school, as it was September. I remembered that I had always wondered if I might be interested in law school, but...

I'm not sure that I said anything else to Coach Fitzsimmons. He was wrong about his choice, I knew that much. He had kept a journeyman veteran over me, a solid player, but I was better. At least that's how I saw it.

This was so inconceivable. I felt sick, and I could feel my face burning, my eyes beginning to well up. I wondered what I would say to my family and friends. I felt like I was in some kind of free fall, headed toward a future that I couldn't even conceive. Actually, no kind of future at all, as far as I was concerned. Of more immediate concern right then was getting out of his hotel room before I started to cry.

My bags were mostly packed in my hotel room, as I had kept everything together in anticipation of heading back to Atlanta with the team shortly. I looked around the hotel room, trying to gather any loose items I had left lying around. My stomach was in knots, and I was having trouble thinking clearly.

I knew this was a disaster. That much I could focus on.

The Hawks intern drove me to the Savannah airport, where the franchise would finish its obligations to me with a one-way flight back to DC. He had made these trips before. Now he was taking me. We traveled in silence, the shimmering heat before us, the deafening silence of defeat—my defeat—engulfing us.

The plane trip home was silent. At least no one else on the plane knew what had just happened. It was not supposed to be like this.

Once I arrived home, I could still smell the stench of defeat all around me. Despite being twenty-two years old, a Harvard graduate, and having to share a bedroom with three younger brothers and a young uncle, I walled myself up in the house for the next two weeks.

Somewhere way down deep inside me, maybe I knew things would get better. I wanted to believe that something else I was supposed to do would begin to surface. I know now that God was still there, even in my discouragement, whether I was aware of His presence or not. He is there in our good times and our bad, I know now.

But at that moment, I was without direction, and without the energy or inclination to think about anything else. Between anger, feeling sorry for myself, and crying, I didn't have any free time.

It wasn't supposed to end this way.

CHAPTER 2

ROOTS AND SACRED TRUSTS

*You don't choose your family. They are
God's gift to you, as you are to them.*

Bishop Desmond Tutu

It was 2004 and there I was, a broadcaster on national
television every week, and suddenly I found myself unable
to speak a single word. Speechless, my family and friends
would say, for the first time in their recent memory.

I can stand in front of crowds full of total strangers, audi-
ences made up of well-known personalities and dignitaries,
or even in front of television monitors knowing that people
beyond the farthest reaches of my imagination are watching
in living rooms, restaurants, community centers, and a variety of other venues, and yet, I was so emotional I couldn't

get out…a…single…word…for what seemed like a minute. I composed myself and spoke from my heart tenderly what my Mom meant to me.

She went by a variety of names: Mrs. Brown, Ma Brown, or Mother Brown. To her friends she was Mary Ann.

To me she has always been Mom.

And now we were gathered together to celebrate Mom on the event of her seventieth birthday and, more importantly, we wanted to give thanks for God mercifully giving Mom back to us after she had gone into code blue the previous year. We had decided to put all of our finery on display to honor her in a loving, intimate way, with HER making the final decisions. The family was in black tie and formal attire, and I had watched with admiration as my siblings, family members, and lifelong friends, spoke to her and about her. My sister had time-lined the whole celebration and wanted us to be mindful of the time, because of Mom's health and the need to get her back home and to bed before the hour got to be too late. All of the comments were very touching. And so, when it was my turn to speak, it was very difficult.

There were too many memories.

At heart, I am truly a mama's boy.

This book is as much about and a product of my parents, and specifically my mother, as it is a story of anything else. I was born in the southeast part of the District of Columbia, but most of my childhood memories are from times after we moved in the late 1950s, when I was around eight or nine years old, in third grade, into the home I grew up in near Catholic University, in the northeast section of DC. It was a modest home in a solidly middle-class neighborhood that was simple, and like most neighborhoods back then, it was safe. It was a neighborhood that had been predominantly white, but now integration was taking hold, and the face of the neighborhood was slowly changing. After we moved in, with some other black families following behind, the white families began to leave.

My father, John Brown, reminded me of Joseph, the husband of Mary, in the New Testament. He was the breadwinner, the backbone of the family, dutifully obedient to the role that he felt that he was committed to play as the head of the household. I remember my father working two and three jobs to provide for Mom and the five of us children, allowing my mother to stay home and raise us. He quietly went about his work, providing a good example of what a strong father looked like while my mother took the primary hands-on role in raising the children.

My father was actively involved in the lives of his wife and children. Despite being busy with his multiple jobs, he was always there for us. He was a taxicab driver, a corrections officer at a local jail (a now closed DC correctional institution housed in Lorton, Virginia), at Avis Rent A Car, a car wash attendant, and a longtime post office employee—all the while caring for five children. He worked long, hard hours, and modeled for us what it meant to support your family as a loving, guiding father. I know that he would have preferred to be with us even more than his hard work to support us permitted. He was always there for our important occassions, making as many sporting events as possible.

When my father spoke, we moved—actually, we jumped. John Brown didn't have to say anything to us twice. What he said was the law, as it was with my mom. They demanded and received our respect, without fail. At times, what he said was catchy. He had axioms that he would trot out and leave with us: "Every good-bye is not gone," and "Every shut-eye is not sleep." Things that were pretty tough to puzzle over if you were just twelve. And he'd simply leave it out there— without explanation—for us to ponder. He always seemed very wise.

My father was from the Georgetown area of Washington, and had been in the army. He served during the beginning of the Korean War just before my birth in February 1951, and continued later as a member of the Army Reserves.

When I ran across my birth certificate in our house, I noticed, with surprise, that my dad's occupation at that time was "car wash attendant." And as I thought about how my family was living in a nice middle-class neighborhood, it was my first introduction to a lesson which would never leave me—how you start in life doesn't have to be how you finish.

As for Mom, well, to me she was much larger than any single character. Mom was our Rock of Gibraltar, as strong a woman as you'd ever find.

My parents were a very sociable pair, at least early on in their marriage when I was a young boy. I remember a lot of activity, a number of gatherings of friends, many of them my father's army buddies. For me, those experiences under-scored the importance my parents placed on camaraderie and the beauty of friendship. They embodied the concept of togetherness for me and my sister and brothers, and gave us a lasting example of how two people should be together—for each other, their family, and others.

When I say that I'm a mama's boy, I don't mean it in the usual pejorative sense that gets bandied about. She was one of the strongest people I know, a woman of strength, integrity, and character, of resolve and courage. I saw firsthand, especially in her later life, how she lived according to God's Word, reading from her Bible each day, and exhibiting for us the way our lives should be lived.

My mother and father were responsible for training us and shaping us morally. We like to say, they had PhD's in Common Sense. Our home was a place of joy and together-ness, a sanctuary for the Browns where we knew that we were always loved. It was also a place of great wisdom—which I began to appreciate later in life—as my mother would share lessons with us straight from God's Word, around the family dining room table.

There were five of us children and later her younger brother Clifton that she took seriously the responsibility to rear and nurture into productive members of society: John, Alicia, Terence, Clifton, Everett, and myself. John is eigh-teen months younger than I am, Alicia three years, Terence and Clifton five, and Everett is eight years younger than me. She must have had her hands full dealing with us, and she might have felt that way, but we never thought that was the case. It always appeared to us that everything was running smoothly and that Mom was completely in control of whatever was happening. When Mom, the Sergeant, spoke, we saluted. It was always "yes ma'am, no ma'am."

All six of us had chores to do—my specialties were ironing the dress shirts, waxing the floors, and washing the windows. The house was always spotless. Mom's mission was to be a homemaker. As a young wife and mother her greatest joy was taking care of her family. She was also able to put her gifted mind to the greatest use possible—raising her children.

All of us kids have had our challenges along the way, and as an adult her response has always been the same: first, look to the Bible to see what guidance it gives for what we were going through. Not what *she* thought was right or wrong, but what did God say about it. Then she'd move on to the next step. She would begin praying for you and the situation. There was many a time that we were not sure how things worked out the way they did, other than to look to my mom and know that her prayers were answered. You always knew that she loved you, whether you were in the right or the wrong. Her love knew no bounds or conditions, although she wasn't shy about letting you know when she thought you were outside of God's perfect and pleasing will—or outside of *her* will for that matter! She never wanted us to stay where we were—if she felt it was outside of God's will—that's how much she loved us.

*　　*　　*

Mom also demonstrated her love for us over meals. I think it was the Southerner in her to do all the cooking, but as a result, I'm a horrible cook. She always showered us with her love, often in the form of meals or snacks. Her desserts—cakes, pies, banana pudding—were legendary. You never left hungry. In fact, you never left unless you were bursting at the seams. I have fond memories of our Sunday family dinners, a tradition that we continue to this day. She would cook abundant amounts of food—chicken or turkey, sweet potatoes, green beans, or lima beans, and on and on. The table would be filled end to end with bowls and platters of the food she created with love. Everything would be ready shortly after we returned from church, and everything would be ready at once. I can't even get one thing ready (on time or otherwise), so some of that feat is lost on me, but I'm told by my wife and sister that having the parts of a meal always hot and ready at once is no small accomplishment—and she did it every single week for a family of seven. (So, not being a competitive athlete anymore, I hope that you will have mercy when you hear about my ongoing challenge with my weight!)

My parents always expected me, as the eldest of five kids, to be the leader and set the right example for my brothers and sister. Although my father worked two and three jobs so that my mother could stay home with us, there was a time when I was older that my mom had a seasonal job around Christmas, and I was expected to be at home and in charge and have everybody pull together around the house.

I was also expected to be in charge when my parents went out for the evening, once they decided that I was old enough to stay with the others. Terence says that I was "quite a comedian," but I simply recall doing whatever was necessary to keep smaller children occupied. I dressed up as Superman or invented stories of characters and faraway places—whatever I needed to do to spin those plates and keep everybody happy until the adults arrived back at the house. My brothers and sister remember far better than I— I must have blocked it out—about one particular Saturday evening when I was a teenager, and Mom and Dad left me in charge so they could go out.

That fateful night, my siblings recall my allowing them to watch the television horror show *Chiller Theatre*, which came on Saturday nights around 11:30. There were only two problems with my decision: one, they were supposed to go to bed by 8:30; and two, we weren't allowed to watch *Chiller Theatre*. As the show was on, a violent thunderstorm blew through our area, with howling winds, thunder, and lightning. By the time my parents arrived home, every light in the house was back on as well as the television. And they found all of us upstairs, hiding under one of the beds. I had not exactly fulfilled the role they had envisioned for me as the leader of the kids.

I was reprimanded. I do recall that particular part of the evening pretty well, even if the rest is a bit hazy.

*　　*　　*

Between the two of them, my parents had very clear ideas of the roles for their children. My mother and father were a product of their era, and gender roles and responsibilities were certain in their minds. My brothers and I were always responsible for taking out the trash, mowing the lawn, and shoveling snow—Alicia never had to help with any of those chores. On the other hand, however, she alone had to do all of the dishes, every day.

As best as I can tell, everyone functioned according to Mom's plan! As for exactly what she did...she did everything...it was yeoman's work and without her things would not have run as smoothly or efficiently. I do know that. If we were getting up for school at seven, by my best estimate she was up by five, making breakfast, packing lunches, and ironing our clothes—we were always clean and neat. As I have said, we had a very nice, modest house which we all proudly called home. All that we owned was clean, in good working order, and tidy. Very tidy.

My parents ran the house like a military base, assigning us chores and then inspecting the tasks once completed. Every morning we were required to make our beds and sweep any dust out from under our beds before we went to school.

Saturday mornings were for housework. Alicia sometimes wonders how Mom came up with some of the jobs she came up with for all of us to accomplish, given how clean the house always remained, but selecting my job was easy—it never seemed to change. Every Saturday morning, along with one or more of my brothers, I had to wash and wax the hardwood floors in our house—and all the floors in the house were hardwood. We were on our hands and knees to do it, and would take turns—one of us would put the wax on while another would take the wax off with a hand buffer.

I used to help Mom with my younger siblings. When Everett was still an infant, I was taking him down the steps in our house, which were, of course, freshly waxed, and I was wearing socks. I slipped on the stairs while carrying Everett but clung to him, though the fall caused a gash on the bridge of his nose (the scar is still there today). To this day, he blames those waxed floors, but points out that because of that fall, he's still my favorite brother. I'll never admit to it in front of John or Terence, though.

Mom was a disciplinarian, whether with us or with other children. Guidelines for appropriate behavior were clear, as were the consequences for any diversion from them. She was one of those parents who was always willing to tell you when you were messing up, even if you weren't her child. Mom never cared what others' backgrounds were, or their race or religion. She cared about what kind of person you were, and whether you were doing what you were supposed to do.

She didn't put up with any foolishness from her children, that much was for certain. She was an advisor and mentor for others at the church and from the neighborhood, but she was a parent to us. My parents expected a great deal from us academically—to do our best and put in whatever effort was required to hit that standard. Even if, however, we were not capable—as opposed to willing—to make the grades, they still had high expectations for us. My mother would say "If you can't bring an A in any other subject I expect an A in citizenship and effort." That is, we could control our disposition, our behavior, and our hunger to excel. And she expected as much from each of us.

My parents were very stringent about where they would let us go and with whom they would let us consort. There were embarrassing—to me—times when I was not allowed to go with someone because my parents either didn't know their parents or weren't comfortable with where we were going. If I was allowed to go, I had to call when I arrived, leave a telephone number at which I could be reached, and always—always—adhere to my curfew, which usually made me the first to have to go home. The flip side of that, however, was that everyone was welcome at our house, so we always seemed to have a crowd at home with us. In addition, if I was allowed to go somewhere, it seemed as though other parents would follow my mom's lead—that is, if Mrs. Brown was letting James go, it must be alright.

Two of the kids who were often in those crowds at our house were Louis Washington and his little brother Alan. Shortly after we moved into our neighborhood, the Washington family moved in behind us. Mr. and Mrs. Washington had two sons, both of whom were younger than me. Louis, their oldest—we all called him Beanie, for reasons none of us ever understood—was three years behind me in school, and ended up going to DeMatha as well. Both of them, as well as

many other children from around the neighborhood, con-
gregrated at our house. I'm not sure exactly what caused that,
but I know that my mom played a large role. It was interesting that she could be strict and lay down firm rules for us
and other kids, yet we all seemed to welcome that. Probably
because most of the other parents were the same way! We
might have protested—and meant it—but deep down there
was probably a part of us that appreciated the boundaries,
knowing that they cared enough to set them. Even though
we might have objected at times, there was a sense of security we all felt in knowing that they were always there watching and expecting us to do what was right as they laid out
that standard.

Mom certainly didn't want to hear what I had to say about
how I wanted to wear my hair. As I got older, afros were
becoming more popular. Each time I would go to the barber
and try to return with something resembling the beginning
stages of an afro, she sent me back. One time in particular, I
was bound and determined to have it longer than I usually
did. She sent me back three times that day, as I recall, each
time to have it cut shorter from the point I'd had the barber
previously leave it.

One experience helped me to understand the wisdom in
keeping my "fro" only moderately long. I had intentionally
put my hair in braids so that when I had the braids taken
out, my hair would be a lot fuller, a lot higher. A bigger "fro."
I did that in preparation for a date one evening. My hair was
nice and high and full. I had just gone past the front porch

when I felt something fall from a tree into my hair. I went back into the house to get my "pie rake" and carefully comb my hair with an upward or outward stroke. I heard something drop into the sink and saw a huge spider! Needless to say, from that point forward, I had what my friends called a "teenie-weenie fro."

My brother John loves to tell the story about the time that he came back to visit Mom, after he was an adult living in San Antonio. He had traveled to the DC area and spent the duration of his time running from place to place, visiting with friends. He never made it back to her house, and when he returned to San Antonio Mom let him know that behavior was unacceptable. A year later he returned, and in his way of telling it, he set an afternoon aside to make sure that he was with Mom. He came into her room—she was ill and in bed—and sat by the bed in a rocking chair, quietly. John said that they passed the time together in silence, mother and son, not needing to talk, just enjoying the simple pleasure of each other's company. At the end of the afternoon, they said their good-byes and John left.

He was recounting this story to others in front of Mom some time later, telling them about what a pleasure the afternoon had been for them, when Mom interjected.

"John, I didn't have the heart to tell you this before," she said. "But about two minutes after you arrived, I fell asleep and didn't wake up until you woke me by saying 'Good-bye.'"

Mom was going to make sure that not only would her

family visit, but they would not make it an afterthought. Or try to squeeze her into an afternoon. Family, for her, came first.

Mom's family—specifically, her father—has always fascinated me. Mom was a product of Hattiesburg, Mississippi, and my grandfather was one of the prominent black businessmen of that era. She had ministers in her family as well as a grandmother who was a missionary, but the one whose stories I've always found myself irresistibly drawn toward is her father, Milton Barnes, Sr.

My grandfather had a ninth grade education, and yet owned a number of businesses in Mississippi, including a baseball team, the Hattiesburg Black Sox. Former Major League pitcher, Mudcat Grant, and others used to tell me that they remembered barnstorming down there and playing the Black Sox in Hattiesburg. I remember Granddaddy telling me, about ten years ago, stories about Hank Aaron and Cool Papa Bell coming to town to play in Hattiesburg, and what great players they were. But the most fascinating story was about Satchel Paige. I remembered folks telling me about one of Mr. Paige's many weapons being the hesitation pitch, where he would start into his throwing motion, actually *stop* in forward stride a second, continue with the pitch, and then deliver the ball to the plate with some "heat" on it. Granddaddy said that was absolutely true. And I remember when an aging Satchel Paige was finally allowed to play with the Major Leagues, that formidable pitch of his was outlawed.

Granddaddy had a fondness for luxury vehicles that he

used to drive from Mississippi to New York, and he would stay at the Hotel Theresa, a black hotel that housed many of the famous black Americans of the time, the "Waldorf Astoria of Harlem," when he would go to watch the World Series, or take in other Negro League games. Granddaddy had story after story of Satchel Paige and others, and I regret that I didn't take Julian Bond's advice. Bond was a colleague when I hosted *America's Black Forum*, a public affairs program. At one point, when he was the head of the NAACP, Julian told me that I really needed to have someone go see Granddaddy and record his wonderful stories. I regret now that I never did it before he passed away, and so behind-the-scenes details of stories, like his being instrumental in bringing a young Martin Luther King, Jr., to town to register blacks to vote and the resulting furor, are lost to fading memories. He was a real mover behind the scenes who had garnered the respect of both the white and black establishment. Mr. Bus Cook, whose prestigious client list includes former NFL quarterback Brett Favre, handled legal work for Granddaddy as well.

Although the baseball team may have been the most high-profile part of Granddaddy's holdings, he also had a nightclub named the Hi Hat, which was one of the "chitlin circuit," nightclubs that were safe for African-American performers in the South. The Hi Hat drew a number of black acts including Ike and Tina Turner, Bobby "Blue" Bland, Little Milton, Moms Mabley, and B.B. King, among others. Oh, and James Brown played there, too. The other James Brown. And then Granddaddy would get up on Sunday morning and head to church fulfilling his responsibilities as a church officer.

In fact, when B.B. King was recognized by the Governor of Mississippi, he sent a limousine the ninety miles down from Jackson, the capital, to Hattiesburg, to bring my grandfather to the event and share in the day with him. B.B. once told me that "back in the day" when very few clubs would allow him to play, my grandfather gave him a grand stage to play on, a time that was instrumental in helping him to build his persona and popularity.

Granddaddy also owned a couple of trucks for shipping, a construction company, a land development company, a dry cleaning business, and had business interests in New Orleans as well. The dry cleaners that he owned was the first black-owned dry cleaners in the state of Mississippi, which he won in a craps game in 1936. Not how I would suggest starting out, but I suppose it was a different world back then, in many ways. Granddaddy actually formed a joint venture with a white-owned dry cleaners that had a contract with a military base in the area. Granddaddy could do the work for half the cost of the other cleaners, who would then send the items to the base. Under the existing contract, everyone was coming out ahead. When the owner of the other cleaners eventually exited the business, he assigned the contract to my grandfather. It was too early in our nation's history for joint ventures between the races in southern Mississippi, but Granddaddy was quite a business pioneer.

He had an amazing entrepreneurial spirit, and I have looked back on my life and some of the risks I have taken and some of the endeavors I have started, and feel that I have some of that spirit of Milton Barnes, Sr., as well. It seemed that every time we went down there to visit, we learned that "Mr. Milton" had a hand in whatever business establishment into which we happened to wander.

—⊶⊷—

Mom did hold a variety of seasonal positions around the holidays, and later when we entered private high schools, she began working fulltime. It was always gratifying to see her able to use her intellect and administrative skills in the outside world. In those positions, she would often end up quickly being promoted, and on many occasions store managers and owners would take the opportunity to go to her for ideas on how to improve areas of the business: inventory control or tracking, organizational issues, and the like. In fact, at one of her positions, the department store sent all of the trainees from around the city to her store, where she was the department manager, for training. She was later promoted to the downtown DC office to become an assistant buyer, even though she wasn't sure she wanted to be promoted to a location so far from home.

She clearly had a great deal of common sense and business sense, no doubt obtained, in large part, through her father. She grew up having to open the cleaners in the morning and close it on some evenings, and had the opportunity in so many disparate business areas to learn how to run a successful enterprise no matter the circumstances or obstacles before you.

Mom was unquestionably a successful employee, one whose work ethic was *never* questioned, but much of her life she was focused on a different type of success. I remember her talking about Joshua 1:8, the Bible verse that she would point to for her understanding of success. "This book of the law shall not depart out of thy mouth; but thou shalt meditate therein day and night, that thou mayest observe to do according to all that is written therein: for then thou shalt make thy way prosperous, and then thou shalt have good success" (KJV). For her, especially as we grew in stature and she grew in her faith, success was not to be measured by a worldly standard, but by following God's will for your life.

Those early years laid the foundation for all of us in becoming engaged members of society. And looking back, I can see that I was beginning to be shaped in what was truly important, in what it really meant to be successful by using your role, whatever that was, to impact those around you—for good.

There are so many memories. Thank God.

CHAPTER 3

HALL OF FAME
INFLUENCE

Think twice before you speak, because your words
and influence will plant the seed of either success
or failure in the mind of another.

Napoleon Hill

I was not an overnight success in sports. I was a good athlete, and a basic level of proficiency in sports came fairly easily, but not stardom. Before high school, I made my basketball team in eighth grade not because I was a great player, but because I was a good listener and the coach loved the fact that I paid attention and he knew I was going to be a hard worker. I was a role player, even then. Unfortunately for me, my role in those days was to set a good example of being a good listener and being coachable—not anything that I did

29

on the court. In fact, on the day when we were introduced to the student body, we dribbled down the court to make a layup—and I blew the wide-open, *uncontested* layup. I still remember the gymnasium full of my peers, laughing. I was looking for a place to hide. Not the way you play it out in your fantasies.

In fact, before I ever became serious about my basketball, my first love was baseball. I still have a picture of me playing Catholic Youth Organization (CYO) baseball when I was fifteen years of age. The picture captures me perfectly at that time, long and lanky, my uniform hanging off me, highlighted by the unique and very prominent nose that is still undeniably mine.

I looked like a human coat hanger.

I hit a substantial number of home runs in the CYO playoffs that summer, and Morgan Wootten, the famed basketball coach from DeMatha Catholic High School in Hyattsville, Maryland, was in attendance. He was there to see a pitcher on our team, a blond-haired guy named Steve Garrett, who threw gas, and was headed to DeMatha to begin the ninth grade the next year. Steve was an exceptional three-sport athlete in football, baseball, and basketball and, to cap it all off, Steve was also a great student. Coach was there to watch the three games in the playoffs, and Steve threw all three of them—a perfect game, a one-hitter and a no-hitter. Coach Wootten felt pretty good about the decision to have Steve attend DeMatha. After the weekend, when Steve's leverage with DeMatha couldn't have been any higher, Steve brought Coach Wootten over to meet me. "Coach, this is our left fielder, James Brown." Coach greeted me and asked if I played basketball also, since I was such a big kid. I did, I told him. "I scored one point last season for my eighth grade team."

He was so impressed that he offered, "I'll talk with the baseball coach for you."

My parents were ecstatic, as it was a private school that I was able to attend for the princely sum of $400 a year, a very stiff price tag back then! And although it was in Maryland, it was located only a few miles outside of DC. Before I arrived at DeMatha, though, I attended Coach Wootten's summer basketball camp because I knew I needed help with my skills to progress on the basketball court. I so took everything he said to heart about spending time on sharpening my skills that I quit playing baseball and focused exclusively on basketball from that time forward.

I'm sure my dad was crushed, although he never said anything to me. Family legend maintains that my father stood over my crib with his brother, my uncle, admiring my right arm and dreaming of the day that I would be an ace pitcher. I hated to disappoint him, but I found that, even during that summer of hitting home run upon home run in CYO baseball, I had no future. Steve Garrett and his heat-seeking missile of a fastball helped me come to that realization. I was sure his fastball was truly "heat-seeking," anyway. And to make matters worse, he had a big, sharp breaking curve ball.

I remember vividly standing in the batter's box during an intra-squad game, waiting for him to throw to me the pitches

I'd seen him throw to opposing batters so many times. He threw me a breaking ball—I read the spin of the pitch coming out of his hand. As usual, he started the pitch inside, coming at the hitter—in this case, me. I was talking myself through it. "It's gonna break. Wait for it, it's about to break. It's gonna break. Isn't it going to break? Is it going to break? IT'S NOT GOING TO BREAK!" my brain screamed, as I hit the dirt, skinny arms and legs flying in every direction.

It broke over the plate for a strike.

That's when I realized that I didn't have the heart to stand in the batter's box as I got bigger and guys started throwing harder and harder. Steve and his breaking ball—they conspired to get me out of the game.

But basketball summer camp was different. I soaked up every pearl of wisdom from Coach Wootten during that camp, every drill he taught, every axiom he conveyed. My becoming one of the best leapers in the District was because I was compulsive about doing the exercises that I had been told would improve my jumping ability—and they did.

My ninth grade year I started on the JV team at DeMatha as Coach felt that even though I had the talent, I needed more refinement before I would be a contributing member of the squad. I kept practicing. My sophomore year I played regularly on the varsity at DeMatha, which was, as far as I was concerned, a huge deal. This was national powerhouse DeMatha! As Coach Wootten pointed out, that didn't happen very often. Even Kenny Carr, who played in the NBA for ten years, played junior varsity his sophomore year at

DeMatha. I kept working and improving, always striving to get better and better and was becoming a complete player. I worked hard on defense, was a shot blocker, great rebounder and leaper, and a good scorer. Coach Wootten has said that my hard work resulted in my being "the total package."

I was also trying to make everyone else better. I was still a good listener, would hit the open man and not worry about my statistics or points, but try to do whatever was requested.

And Coach Wootten was unusual in his method of teaching. He never demanded or yelled to get us to do something. Instead, he always requested. He spoke with authority and conviction in a fashion that you *knew* what he spoke about was right—period. In the four years that I played for him, I never once heard him curse. He is such an outstanding communicator that he is able to find the right vocabulary and inflection to his voice to make his point. He *never* cursed. He made it clear when you were wrong and he corrected you, he exhorted and encouraged, never yelled or demeaned. He figured out how to motivate each player and what buttons to push, without bringing down his own standards for himself in the process.

Coach simply didn't think that it was possible to antagonize and be productive at the same time. That by the mere fact of assaulting and belittling someone, you were not able to positively influence them and be a productive teacher. He had both a short- and long-term view of his players—as players and citizens. And he viewed himself first and foremost as a teacher. In fact, he taught me World History in ninth grade. If he didn't think that cursing was an appropriate way to teach his students in the classroom, he likewise didn't think that cursing at his players was an appropriate way to communicate what he wanted to teach us about basketball. He always told us that he would never knowingly embarrass us, and that if he ever did so, we were to go to him and tell him. Just as he expected us never to embarrass him.

His methods worked. We were good.

We won the Catholic League Championship every year that I was on the varsity, and my junior year we were named National Champions. And as the seasons progressed it was encouraging to know I played a valuable role in that success. In my sophomore year I began to get more and more playing time over the course of the season. I suppose I owe part of the credit for that to my friends. I have always tried to be friendly with a ready smile and kind word—that's how I'm wired. Coach Wootten describes me as "overwhelmingly" the most popular student of the four hundred boys at DeMatha while I was in attendance. He may be exaggerating, but the one thing that I'm sure of is that whatever popularity I had worked in my favor on the basketball court. Students would help me gain playing time with the occasional chant of "We want James!" until I was put in the game.

Coach Wootten made certain that he taught us much more than basketball. He would always ask us if we had worked hard enough over the summer to improve our game. Whoever he asked invariably answered yes, and he would lean in, and ensure that he had their attention.

"Did you really?" A nod would follow, but with a little less affirmation.

"Well, just think about this. Somehow, somewhere out there, there's another player in the city who was paying the price to get better, working two or three or four or five hours per day on the basketball court to sharpen their game, all summer. And if you weren't, and you two meet on the court this season...who do *you* think is going to win?"

"Basketball players are made over the summer."

Once I was in high school, I always came and helped at Coach's summer camps. I was helping out, but also doing whatever I could to improve my game. Coach remembers setting the baskets to eleven feet and that I could still dunk on them. One summer, I had a broken bone in my foot and a cast covering my foot, all the way to my upper shin. I could still dunk, even with the cast. I'm less than certain that's what the doctor recommended.

In fact, Coach often used me to help demonstrate to the campers that they should be very confident about becoming good shooters because the basket was as wide as the ocean. He would then have me take two basketballs and dunk them simultaneously—of course, back then I was only carrying about 185 pounds into flight versus two hundred... and...well...uh...just a bit more weight now...

Coach's big emphasis, as I noted, was that the great players were made in the off-season. That's when you have time to focus on the fundamentals, have a chance to improve your shooting, work on ball handling, become a better defensive player. I was relentless about my off-season preparation, spending several hours every day working on my game, and that contributed greatly to the player that I ultimately became.

Depth before height, once again. Build the foundation. I learned that lesson without realizing it, working hard whether school was in session or out, working to stay ahead of others around the city that I was sure were working just as hard as I was. While others were relaxing, we could be getting better to get ahead. If they were getting ahead, then we'd better be keeping pace by paying the price and sharpening our skills. It was what you did when no one was watching that made all the difference in basketball. Coach made certain we knew that that didn't just apply to what we did on the basketball court. He made it clear that success was much more perspiration than inspiration—and he drilled that home until we realized that he was talking about life, too, not just basketball.

"If one guy works hard all summer to improve and one guy is haphazard in his off-season approach, when they meet on the court of battle the next fall, who is going to win?" I think Coach Wootten may have told me that once or twice during my career. Or maybe a hundred times.

"Practice doesn't make perfect, practice makes permanent. Therefore, make sure that you are practicing the right way, the right things. Making those right things permanent."

He gave us the four priorities in life that he stressed were crucial if we were going to take the court for him at DeMatha High School: God first, family second, our academics next, and finally basketball. Those were our four priorities, in order, if we were to play for him. He made it clear that he required those things because they led to success.

He coached for forty-six years at DeMatha, and is the winningest coach in high school basketball history. With a career record of 1,274 wins and 192 losses, he was inducted into the Basketball Hall of Fame in Springfield, Massachusetts, in 2000, the only coach in the Hall for work exclusively at the high school level. Red Auerbach, the Boston Celtics great coach and president, presented him for induction into the Hall, and I was blessed to attend his enshrinement, representing all of his former players at DeMatha. We won the mythical national championship in 1968, my junior year, and he won more than 30 conference championships in those forty-six seasons. He is truly a legend in coaching circles, and John Wooden has called him one of the best coaches he has ever seen at any level. He is an innovator, as was seen before I arrived, when his team broke Power Memorial Academy's seventy-one-game winning streak in 1965. Trying to prepare his players to play against the sheer size of Power's Lew Alcindor (now known as Kareem Abdul-Jabbar), Coach Wootten, at the suggestion of the school principal, John Moylan, an avid tennis player, had all the players on defense hold tennis rackets over their heads to get those on offense accustomed to shooting over their rackets, simulating the wingspan of Lew Alcindor.

*   *   *

One of the more important things I received from Coach during my time at DeMatha was beyond the dimensions of the court. One of my main sources of learning—that I should seek to complement and support others' gifts and abilities—came from Coach Wootten. He was a phenomenal coach and teacher of basketball, but even more than that, he understood how to build a team, and to communicate those things that we could apply in any setting. I, of course, didn't realize that at the time, but have drawn on his lessons and axioms for living ever since I have been out of high school.

He always underscored—always—the value of team. We were to be unselfish and put the team before our own interests. He made that very clear with me. Even though others might see me as the team star—a two-time high school All-American, and I would be named the Player of the Year in Washington, DC, for 1969—I had to toe the mark like everyone else. I was one member of the team. I recall having to leave campus one day after school to receive an award. I asked Coach Wootten for permission, because we had practice that afternoon a couple of hours after school ended.

"You can go," he said, "as long as you are back before practice starts."

I returned five minutes late for practice, as I recall, but given that I had a good reason, Coach Wootten didn't even acknowledge my tardiness. We practiced as normal, and as the practice came to a close, I headed out of the gym with the others until I heard Coach's whistle, along with his voice. "JB, you're staying afterwards. You were five minutes late. Get on the line." He then proceeded to have me run sui-cides, in which you start at the end line, sprint to the nearest free throw line, come back to the end line, then to half court and back to the end line, then to the farther free throw line and back, and finally to the far end line and back. At each turn, you've got to reach down and touch the court.

After one of those, I had to run a lap around the gym. As I was running, I saw the other players taking notice as they headed into the locker room. His whistle communicated clearly: no one was above the team.

He wasn't finished with me. Then I had to do push-ups, twenty-five of them. At this point, I had gone through a full practice, then run sprints and a lap, and my arms were burn-ing and shaking. And tight. But Coach Wootten offered me a way out of further discipline.

"Go to the free throw line. If you can make five out of five, you're done."

I could barely lift my arms to shoot—my arms felt flaccid. The first shot fell about ten feet short of the basket, and he directed me back to the end line. Sprints. Around the gym. Push-ups.

"Back to the free throw line. Make five in a row and you're outta here."

This shot was worse than the first.

"Back on the [end] line!" Sprints, a lap, push-ups. After four circuits—and no, I didn't make one free throw along the way—he told me that was enough, get a shower.

There were two lessons that day. The first was that I was to be on time. I had a commitment to the team, and anything else—even awards—would have to come outside of the time dedicated to my team obligations. We were all to share his team philosophy and embody it. Be there. Mean what you say. Be accountable and responsible.

The second lesson was mercy. If it weren't for Coach Wootten's mercy, I would still be doing the circuit. There was no way in the world that I was ever going to make a free throw, let alone five in a row.

While watching film, Coach Wootten would always make a big to-do over the pass that *led* to the great shot. He wouldn't focus on the shot, but would stop the film and make sure that we'd all seen the pass that led to it—repeatedly. "The shot may be what the crowd cheered for and what the writers wrote about, but it was the *pass* that made it all possible." Then, he would stop and compliment the guy who set the pick that allowed another to make the pass that, finally, led to the great shot. The pick and the pass were necessary—just as necessary as the shot. In fact, without them, there would have been no shot.

It was all about team. The guy who scrambled all over the court and dived for a loose ball on the floor, knocking it out of bounds, would never make it into the box score for that play. However, Coach would stop the film—again, an example of what he believed was critical to our success as a team.

We were each a significant and integral part of the team. Each of us brought certain gifts and abilities to the whole of the team. The team might be successful on the back of one player or another for a game or two—but over the long haul it was a collection of individuals joined for a common cause—each filling the *roles* which brought out the best of the team.

It's all about what we all bring to the table to make the other guys look good. He would compliment me as much for my position and effort on a rebound as he would for me tapping the ball back into the basket for a score. He taught me, and I truly began to believe, that you always do the little things, the things that the world may not recognize, but that those in the know—your teammates, your coaches, those who understand the game—would appreciate the importance of: fighting for the rebound, getting up in traffic to tap in a missed shot, getting to the free throw line, doing the tedious work that really set the tone for the team.

He taught us to be role players, to put team above ourselves and our interests.

Looking back, it really is impressive how well Coach Wootten instilled in us the value of team. I can remember my performance in very few individual games, but can remember every one of my teammates and the overall experience we had together. I may have received a Most Valuable Player award and made the all-tournament team when playing against Long Island Lutheran, but my recollection is that we trailed by a huge deficit, battled back in a charge that I played my part in, only to lose at the wire. It's a tribute to Coach's teachings that I have a nagging sense that *I* played really well and may have been recognized for that, but since the *team* didn't win, it wasn't ever something that I thought back upon.

*　　*　　*

During my last couple of years at DeMatha, the Washingtons from our neighborhood began attending our games.
Their oldest son Louis was three years behind me, so they
were clearly coming just to be supportive of me, and I appreciated that. Mrs. Washington always had the family remain
after the game to greet me, and she said that Mr. Washington
would protest that I was a young man with lots of friends,
and didn't need to be bothered with them. But I did. I was
grateful for their support and glad they stayed at the gym to
visit.

Once, during my senior year, we went to play Johnstown
Catholic High School in Johnstown, Pennsylvania. I was our
returning All-American, and was averaging over twenty-one
points a game, as I recall. I had a horrible first half. We came
into the locker room and we were trailing. Coach Wootten
walked in, looked at me, and didn't say a word. It was a ten-
minute halftime and he was silent for the first five minutes
of that halftime, staring at us, staring at me.

Finally, he took the halftime statistics sheet that he had
been handed when he entered the locker room. "Let's see..."
he said, as he followed his index finger down the page, staring intently at the numbers. "Let's see how my All-American
superstar did in the first half. Let's see: Brown. There it is."
His face lit up. "Great! Wow! Two points! One rebound!
That's great!"

He looked up at me, the excited expression gone. "Tell
you what, *Mary* Brown. Go out there and do that again the

second half. Just double it for me. That's all I ask. Just finish this game for us with four points and two rebounds. Can you do that for me? Just think, if she can go out there and play hard, she could probably go do that again, and finish with two rebounds and four points. Can you do that for them?" He gestured to the other players, assembled in the locker room, staring at me.

His goal was not to demean, but to get under my skin and light a fire. And it worked. I still can hear him: "Mary Brown." I went out in the second half and destroyed the other team. I had fifteen or sixteen rebounds in the second half and eighteen points. We won. But only because I had risen to my commitment to the others and met my obligations to the team.

At the end of my senior year we played in the Knights of Columbus tournament. It was a tournament featuring the top Catholic schools from all over the eastern United States, plus some outstanding public school programs. My senior year we lost only one regular season game, to McKinley Tech at Cole Field House on the University of Maryland campus. They had a great team and beat us badly—by about fifteen.

We had reached the semifinals of the Knights of Columbus tournament, and I was in the throes of college recruiting. I had been getting calls very late at night, keeping up with my studies, going on recruiting trips, and still working hard at basketball. I was worn out.

Coach Wootten has always had a policy that you can take yourself out of the game when you are tired, and once out, you may put yourself back in when you're ready. His thinking was that by allowing guys to put themselves back in will serve as an incentive for them to remove themselves when truly tired, knowing that they can go back in when they are ready.

I took myself out of the semifinal game against St. Thomas More, with Ernie DiGregorio, who would later play at Providence College and in the NBA, as their star. I sat next to Coach Wootten, who always keeps the seat next to him for whoever just came out, so he can talk with us about what is occurring out there and instruct us as he sees fit. I proceeded to collapse into his lap. They took me to Providence Hospital, which is near my home, where I was admitted and spent the night, suffering from exhaustion. I was ruled out for the following day's game, the championship game of the KOC tournament, against McKinley Tech.

My teammates took my warm-up jacket and laid it over a chair that they had kept empty on the bench for the afternoon for me, and before a packed house, my team went on to beat McKinley Tech by twenty-two points and win the tournament. It was a tribute to how good we were, and how well Coach Wootten infused us with a sense of team, that we were able to win that game. There were those who thought that the thirty-seven point swing in our favor, simply by not having me in uniform, was too big to ignore—but I prefer to think that my teammates were talented, and maybe were playing hard for me as well.

By the way, I startled everyone when I walked down out of the stands for the awards ceremony. I had managed to sneak out of the hospital and find a ride to the gym—I couldn't stand the thought of not being there with my teammates and helping them celebrate.

CHAPTER 4

A HANDSHAKE AND HARVARD

*To educate a man in mind and not in morals
is to educate a menace to society.*

Theodore Roosevelt

My recruitment in 1969 came three years after the great social barrier-breaking event in college basketball: the 1966 National Championship game in which the underdog Texas Western squad and their all-black starting five beat the powerhouse University of Kentucky team, with head coach Adolph Rupp and their all-white starting five (including Pat Riley, president of the Miami Heat). So by the time I was being courted by colleges to play basketball, all schools were recruiting players regardless of their color—even Kentucky offered me a scholarship.

All of us in the Brown family knew we were going to college. It seemed so normal at the time, though, to us that our parents, who did not attend college themselves, would have very firm expectations that we would attend college. They were committed to making sure that their children were educated to their fullest.

As colleges started showing interest in me, Coach Wooten took me aside. Having guided hundreds of players through the recruiting process and in securing college scholarships, he wanted to make certain that I clearly understood all the aspects of the process, which was another world altogether from anything normal. As the first to go to college in my family, his advice was necessary and greatly appreciated.

"When you visit a school," he told me, "they're going to show you the best of everything. They set you up, by design, in the perfect honeymoon situation. Therefore, you cannot commit when you are on campus. Leave the school and come home. If you still feel the same way after twenty-four hours, then commit."

Coach wasn't kidding. I was wined and dined with every visit. Nice accommodations, lobster (which I love), and other fancy meals, none of which were an issue back when I was eighteen and six-five and two hundred and ten pounds. I have to be a little more careful with the drawn butter these days.

During one of those visits, I decided to call Coach from Chapel Hill, home of the University of North Carolina. I had just finished a great visit with Coach Dean Smith, and loved the school, the players I had met and everything I knew about their program. I also admired Coach Smith—not only for the success that he had and the way he treated his players—but how well all of his ex-players were doing in various professions. He also was exemplary for his approach to civil rights. Although it was still a tumultuous time for race relations in our country, Coach Smith had already done a great deal to further the rights for all races in North Carolina, using his particular platform as head basketball coach at a university as respected as was the University of North Carolina. I told Coach Wootten that I wasn't going to commit on campus, but UNC was where I wanted to attend school. And I told him why. We agreed that I should tell Coach Smith that I was ninety-nine percent sure that I would attend, but needed to go home and speak with my family.

When I got home, I found out that a letter from Harvard University had arrived, and was sitting on Coach Wootten's desk. For my mom, dad, and myself, once that letter had been placed in our hands, any dilemma for the Brown family concerning which college I would attend had effectively and decisively ended. I had admired Bill Bradley, the Princeton great, who was then playing for the Knicks. The impact he had on me, being an excellent student and athlete, was tremendous. Who knows—if the Princeton letter had come first, maybe I would have narrowed it down between UNC and Princeton. As it was, Harvard was immediately elevated to a position on a par with Carolina. But, I knew in my heart Harvard would be my choice. I felt that if I could qualify for admission and enjoyed athletic success, not only would I be fulfilling my parents' dream of getting an excellent education, but maybe it would encourage other African-American athletes to do the same. Mom was very clear—even if it meant that they had to take on additional jobs, or second and third mortgages on the house, which it turns out they did, as my siblings went to school—they would do whatever it took for me to be able to attend Harvard.

Shortly thereafter, Harvard did what most schools do in wooing talent: roll out a high profile alumnus. Harvard had one that Carolina couldn't match—Ted Kennedy. The senator contacted Coach Wootten and arranged for us to go to Capitol Hill to meet him. We visited with Senator Kennedy in his office, watched him cast a couple of votes in the Senate, and before the day was out, I promised him that I would visit Harvard before deciding.

Red Auerbach, the legendary Boston Celtics coach and front office executive, was a great friend of DeMatha High and Coach Wootten. Even he weighed in on my college choice. Well, kind of. He grinned at me and told me, "James, remember this: there is only one Harvard." He didn't tell me where to go, but he did leave it at that. I got the message. From my mom to respected politicians to basketball executives—everything was beginning to look Crimson. My family remembers Ted Kennedy coming by the house and the impression it made on them. But as impressive as the Senator was, the two alumni who had the most influence on me were Clifford Alexander and Barrett Linde. Cliff was the former Secretary of the Army in the Jimmy Carter Administration and Linde, a wealthy Washington, DC, builder, really connected with me.

It was still a tough decision because of how much I liked Chapel Hill, Coach Smith, and realizing that the University of North Carolina was an excellent school as well.

In the meantime, Coach Wootten called me into his office. "James, how many schools do you plan on enrolling at next year?" I looked at him, confusion on my face. "That is the fifth call I've gotten from a coach—North Carolina, Maryland, Michigan—who tells me that you're '99 percent sure' that you're coming to his school."

I grimaced.

"James, you're going to learn, at some point in your life, to tell somebody no."

Weeks later I was still wrestling with the decision. I lost track of who had contacted me and what I had said to whom because of the magnitude of the overall numbers, but my siblings have said that I was being recruited by upward of two hundred schools. Letters were coming in every day from all parts of the country, and I was still unable to decide.

Mom and Dad never pressured me, repeatedly saying the decision was mine. Mom and Dad just couldn't get past Harvard, though. None of us could. Coach Auerbach was right—there is only one Harvard. And Mom was very concerned with what college offered the most for my future. She taught me over the years about the value of education. "What if you break your leg and can't play basketball again?

If you go to Harvard, you'll always have a great education as your foundation." She was often fond of saying that "whatever you put between your ears, no one can ever take away."

In fact, Mom had a classic encounter with Coach Wootten one day during my tenth grade year. I was playing both junior varsity and varsity at the time, which I explained to Mom was quite an honor. "If it cuts into your homework time here at the kitchen table, it will be over," she responded.

One fateful day, it did.

I didn't return home from school when the streetlights came on, which had always been my appointed time to be home and seated at the kitchen table, doing homework. Mom called DeMatha, and reached an assistant basketball coach, who politely explained that Coach Wootten and I weren't available, as practice had continued later than usual, and we were on the floor.

Mom clarified the point. "You're telling me that I can't speak with my son because practice is going on, and further that he's not home doing homework because of that practice? Please let Coach Wootten know that I'm sorry that he's unavailable, but that James won't be a part of the basketball program at DeMatha any further because of the conflict between practice and him getting his studies in."

After a moment's pause, Coach Wootten came on the line. His assistant had re-examined the situation. "Mrs. Brown, I apologize. I agree with you—academics must always come first. James is on his way home, and this will not happen again." To his credit, it was a rarity for this to have happened in the first place, and it did not happen again.

She also helped me to understand the distinction among the scholarships that were offered. Because what Harvard was offering me was need based, all I had to do was to maintain good grades, and I would stay on scholarship there. The criteria for continuing in school depended not on my continuing to play basketball, but on the quality of my grades. If, however, I accepted an athletic scholarship at another school, and sustained a career-ending injury while in school, what my mother and father highlighted was the possibility that the scholarship could be revoked. They were wise to focus on that possibility, regardless of how unlikely it might have seemed to me. I was also still intrigued by the chance to do what Bill Bradley had done (at Princeton), an accomplishment I admired. He had graduated from Princeton in 1965, after a career in which he had been selected as a three-time All-American and had led Princeton to a number three final national ranking following the 1965 NCAA Tournament. He was named the top amateur athlete in the United States in 1965 and it was readily apparent, from Bradley's college career and NBA career which followed with the New York Knicks, that it was certainly possible for another player to be no less successful on the court coming out of an Ivy League school.

I wanted to be an inspiration. I suppose we all do in a way. In addition to every other reason my family had for me to attend Harvard—except for the possible exception of my brother Terence who thought it would be so cool to have a brother who was a Tarheel and therefore was still pulling for UNC and Dean Smith to snatch victory from the jaws of defeat on the recruiting trail—I wanted to be a role model to others, especially those younger kids who had followed my high school career. As a young man growing up in a very modest area of DC, who certainly was not born with a silver spoon in his mouth, I wanted to be a role model for kids from similar backgrounds by showing them that they, too, could rise above their circumstances. Given that it was still the late 1960s, and the country was still wrestling with the aftereffects of Dr. Martin Luther King, Jr.'s tragic death, and the continuing civil rights movement, as well as the ongoing struggle in Vietnam, I thought that maybe there might be kids who saw my going to Harvard as something they could do, too. That the ticket to success was not just in having athletic talent.

By no means am I a charter member of Mensa, and I didn't perform particularly well on standardized tests. What I did, however, was work assiduously at my studies. Where it might take another student thirty minutes to grasp the material, it might take me a little longer. I wasn't fazed, however, by that. I was willing to spend as much time as it took, and knew that I would eventually master whatever material was assigned. And when I ever had a momentary lapse in commitment, I just reflected on how hard my mom and dad were working to make this all possible for me.

After an agonizing and long period of introspection and analysis, the process finally resulted in my selection of Harvard. They offered me early admission, because of my grades and the situation I was in with my recruitment elsewhere, to allow me to effectively end the continuing recruitment process and put it all behind me. I accepted and said that I would attend.

That's when the letter arrived that threw our house into chaos. Any thoughts of being a role model in Cambridge were put on hold when I held in my hands the envelope with "UCLA" written on its face in deep sky blue and sun gold.

"Mom, this is from UCLA. I have to go. I have to at least visit. Pauley Pavilion. John Wooden. It's U-C-L-A." I said it slowly, carefully enunciating each letter, as if she were having trouble with my spelling. "It's the mecca of college basketball. They dominate college basketball—they've won two straight National Championships and four of the last five!"

My mother was unmoved. My father, too, was completely unmoved. They sat me down. "James, you have given your word to Harvard. Your word means more than anything, son. You shook hands and said that you were coming—you cannot change your mind now. You're going to Harvard." That was that.

I told UCLA that I was headed to Harvard, and went up to Cambridge to play for Bob Harrison. Coach Harrison was an NBA All-Star, and had played for the old Minneapolis Lakers, the Milwaukee Hawks, St. Louis Hawks, and Syracuse Nationals. He had come to Harvard a year earlier from Kenyon College, a program that he had turned around, and arrived with great expectations of doing for the basketball program at Harvard what had been done at Princeton and

Columbia. My class came in with great expectations at Harvard, with the thought that we were going to put Harvard basketball on the same path to national prominence those other Ivy League schools had traveled. We were ranked the second-best incoming freshman class in 1969 (freshman couldn't play varsity in those days), and a number eleven had our highest preseason ranking in school history the next year, when we were finally eligible to play. Instead, we were mediocre. My sophomore year, when we finished 11-3 in the Ivy League and had K.C. Jones, the Celtics great, as an assistant coach, was our best season. Coach Harrison was a wonderful person, knew the game well, and was a strict disciplinarian, but for whatever reason, athletic success didn't work out for him, nor us, at Harvard. A number of people pointed the finger at him for our lack of success, but that was unfair. We had as much to do with the lack of success as he did. It was, after all, a *team* effort.

These were politically and socially challenging times—the Vietnam War, the happenings at Kent State and other campuses, the Black Panthers—and I'm of the impression that we didn't handle that transition as well as we might have under different circumstances.

Basketball wasn't a complete loss as a member of the Harvard Crimson. There were some good memories, mixed in among the general feelings of unfulfilled potential. My sophomore year I was surprised by a visit from our neighbors the Washingtons who drove from DC over to Annapolis to see us beat the Naval Academy. It was a special treat for a neighborhood family to show up. They were awfully kind to show up, time after time, whether in high school or college, to support me.

I remember two games from my junior year that stand out in particular. One was a game we played at Boston University a few miles away from our campus in Cambridge. BU had a couple of players who were also from the Washington, DC, area, so it had somewhat of a hometown rivalry feel for me. That was probably my best individual game, as I was in a zone all night, scoring thirty-six points in a 104–77 win for the Crimson. At that time, I was not a great, consistent outside scorer, but I was shooting and scoring from all over the court. It was one of those nights when it seemed that I could take three or four steps across midcourt and shoot—and it would go in. I say "one of those nights," but come to think of it, that was probably the only night of my life like that! Long arching jumpers from all over, and nothing but the bottom of the net. And those thirty-six points came at a time when college basketball didn't have the current three-point line, either.

Of course, with the outfit I chose to wear for the trip to Boston University that day, I had no choice but to play well. We went over to BU's gymnasium and walked around campus for a while. You couldn't miss me. The movie *Super Fly* had just been released that year, and I showed up on BU's campus wearing a white leather full-length coat as if I had stepped right out of the movie. However, to make the coat truly classy, I had selected one with gray faux fur around the hem and the collar. It looked like something Clyde Frazier, the New York Knicks point guard would wear, only he'd have *real* fur, of course. And, naturally, a hat to match. Did I mention the red, zip-up boots, and gray bell-bottom pants? If you're going to do it, do it up right, from head to toe. It really made a statement. I'm not sure *what* the statement was that I was trying to make. And I shuddered later wondering just what that statement was that I was making to the Harvard alumni who traveled across the river to see the game.

It was certainly a different take on the fur coats usually being worn at Harvard games.

The other notable game from my junior year was the one when Oral Roberts came to play at our home court, which was located on the fourth floor of the Indoor Athletic Building (the IAB, we called it, out of sheer Harvard creativity). A capacity crowd of 1,600 was in attendance, and we played a game for the ages. Unfortunately, it ended up with a 100–99 Oral Roberts victory.

My Harvard experience was outstanding and memorable; our lack of success on the court was my only regret—it still pains me to think of our struggles, after the promise with which we entered. We entered with a couple of high school All-Americans and several All-State players, but we could never put it together to turn the program around. I wish I had displayed the same work ethic that I applied both before and after college. Later, after I moved into broadcasting, I had the opportunity to speak with Hubie Brown and Chuck Daly, who were coaches at Duke University and the University of Pennsylvania, respectively, during the time I attended Harvard. Each of them later went on to great success as coaches at the NBA level. They told me how they would get their teams ready to play us, telling their players that we were a team full of radicals. They exhorted their players not only to win for Duke or Penn, but for the entire establishment of the United States and all that it stood for, as we—Harvard—stood on the side of chaos and anarchy. Whatever works, I suppose. I asked Coach Brown and Coach Daly if they realized they were talking about Harvard (sure, it was a chaotic time) but it *was* Harvard. The administration at Harvard was hardly going to let anarchy reign. Hubie and Chuck both smiled and shrugged, indicating agreement, but a shrug that also said they would say and do whatever it took to motivate their teams to beat us, which they did.

My time at Harvard was significant for another reason, though. A reason that would continue from then to now to impact my journey toward the person God wanted me to be. At the time, in addition to fielding all of the challenges of adjusting to college sports and struggling with the off-court challenges on campus which continually seemed to infiltrate from those affecting our society, I was searching spiritually as well. We were good, solid kids, great neighbors, in a good household. My parents' example of how they lived their lives was my yardstick—and as I found out through the years that would follow my childhood—was a good example to emulate. But I found myself inwardly searching for meaning to my life when I was off at college. It was at once an uncomfortable feeling, yet one I knew was causing me to head in a better direction. I remember in Cambridge being drawn to a particular church near campus. I was attracted to the building, I think, more than whatever was going on inside. I felt a lure, and would attend occasionally, but like a map without a legend, I never fully grasped and applied what was being conveyed. I felt a pull and tug on my soul, but I didn't really respond. But the tug continued. Francis Thompson wrote a poem, later edited into a song by Michael Card, called "Hound of Heaven," portraying God as always following us, always after our hearts, always wanting to have a personal relationship with us. He was doing that with me at Harvard. But I was still running—searching, I thought. I had not fully surrendered in every aspect, or in every area of my life. But I was heading in the right direction, and even though I wasn't sure what was happening—I felt comfort in where I was going.

I had arrived at Harvard with so many accolades and didn't have the really strong figure that Coach Wootten had been to harness me and my complacency, and I think I succumbed to all the adulation that came from being an athlete on campus. Even though I had felt I wanted to be a role model to the kids in the neighborhood, I never fully understood that the position I had been given as a college athlete was a platform to influence everyone around me—not just those neighborhood kids—for good or otherwise. I hadn't yet come to a full realization of what it meant to follow Christ and put others first, so I wandered spiritually without a clear direction for an uncomfortably long period. I hadn't yet realized that the platform I had been given was from Him, to use for His purposes, to influence and positively impact others.

Between the times of unrest on campuses and the struggles we all had trying to find athletic success, we simply never fulfilled our full potential as a team. I realized again the burden of potential and the reality of its being as much of a curse as a blessing. At the end of the day, however, the ultimate responsibility lay with me. I knew from high school what it took to be successful. Players are made in the off-season, but when guys from other schools were working all summer getting better, we weren't. We had plenty of excuses available, including those who wanted to argue that the academic course load made it impossible to enjoy sustained basketball excellence at Harvard, but I disagree. We were the problem. Even with all of this I was still hopeful for a career in professional basketball.

A good memory from those times was getting to see my family. My brother, John, attended Curry College in Milton, Massachusetts, just south of Boston. The way my sister tells it, Mom told Alicia that she could go to any school she wanted to—as long as it was in Massachusetts. She chose Emerson College in Boston, which meant that by my senior year, three of us were in school in Massachusetts. What was important to my Mom was that my brother and I could watch over our younger sister. For my youngest brother, Everett, however, who was still at home, this meant a significant number of eight-hour drives with Mom and Dad from DC to Boston to visit us and to see our basketball games. Although he enjoyed being in the locker room and going to the games, Everett said that he had had enough of Boston by the time the three of us finished our Massachusetts educations. I'm not sure it was really anything about Boston as much as the numerous long trips—which he wouldn't miss—that led to Everett's feelings about the area. (Terence, who also was still at home with Mom and Dad and Everett, was so involved in high school athletics and other activities that he often wasn't able to come.) I have always enjoyed having my family nearby, even if it took two of them attending schools near mine, and numerous trips for the others to make it happen. I always felt a bit incomplete when they weren't nearby, but that's the way I have always felt about family and still do to this day.

It made being so far from home much more tolerable. As it was, those four years marked the only time I would live outside of the DC area.

But those times in Cambridge were also times of transition for me. Times of both failing to live up to expectations and learning again why that happened and how not to let that happen again, and they were times of the beginnings of a deeper search for the person God had created me to be. Significant times for many reasons.

And at the end of it all, one other memorable moment occurred. I got my degree—from Harvard University. My parents would have settled for nothing less.

CHAPTER 5

REBOUND

Thou wilt show me the path of life: in thy
presence is fullness of joy; at thy right
hand there are pleasures for evermore.

Psalm 16:11 (NIV)

I signed my forty-thousand dollar a year contract with the Atlanta Hawks—complete with a two-thousand dollar signing bonus, as I recall—and headed off to training camp in Savannah, Georgia. Over the course of that long hot summer, Pete Maravich and I got to be great friends during all the activities of the camp. Not only did Pistol Pete take me under his wing on the basketball court, but we both shared a love of the martial arts, and on weekends we would go to whatever Bruce Lee or other kung fu movies were playing in the area.

Pete and the other star of the team, Lou Hudson, were very complimentary of my game on the court and continually encouraged me to just keep working hard, keep my nose clean and stay out of trouble—they obviously didn't know my mother who had already made all of that crystal clear to me for the last twenty-two years. The guy I was competing with for the final roster spot had not practiced or played nearly as well in camp—in my very objective opinion, and so right up until the moment of my release I thought I would be the guy filling that twelfth roster spot going into the exhibition and regular season.

The last time I had lived at home, I had been packing up, readying myself for a life at Harvard and whatever was beyond. I knew that a season of my life was coming to an end and that I would, more than likely, be living elsewhere from this point forward. Now, though, I had unexpectedly returned home after being released by the Hawks, with no idea what the future might hold. I certainly had no desire to go outside and run into the Washingtons, the Smiths, the Miltons, the Wallaces, or anyone else in the neighborhood.

And so I just hid in my old room. My brother John was still off at college, but my other brothers Terence and Everett, as well as Clifton, were all at home. We had all shared a bedroom growing up, the four of us boys. It was a three-bedroom house that we lived in, and my parents used one, my sister had her own, so the four boys had two sets of bunk beds. And one room. It had always been cozy before—regardless the size, and it was small, four boys sharing it would tend to make it feel cozy—but now I'm sure I was driving my high school brothers crazy, moping and hurting, refusing to leave the house. I stayed that way for the two weeks after my ignominious return.

My parents and my brothers gave me the space I needed and a chance to come to grips with the death of my dream. Upon returning home from getting cut, Mom and Dad were as one would expect parents to be: very supportive, consoling, and encouraging. Mom's repeatedly exhorted me to "get on with becoming a success in the game of life—after all, you went to school to get an excellent education, an education that would provide the necessary foundation for you, in just this instance, when the rug of athletics was snatched from under your feet."

They had patience with me, allowing me to sulk and moan for a period of time, but finally after a couple of weeks they said that it was time to get on with my life. After all, preparation for the rest of my life after basketball was the primary reason I had selected Harvard, they reminded me. I just couldn't imagine anything besides a future in basketball. It was so clear to me that basketball was what I was gifted in, what I was created to do. I was beginning to realize that, for as many years of my life as I could recall, I had always felt as though my identity in the world which knew me, and the world which I knew, was inextricably tied to what I did on the basketball court. Little, if anything else.

Basketball was who I *was*.

When I finally did start to venture out of the house after my self-imposed two-week hibernation, the reaction I received to my sooner-than-planned return from the ranks of the NBA was varied. My friends—doing their best to deflect the tension and embarrassment both they and I were feeling—provided me with a ready-made list of excuses. "Cotton Fitzsimmons had a favorite" (a favorite player, that he kept instead of me and obviously without regard for ability), "the league was too black" (the implication being that the Hawks therefore needed to keep more whites), and so on. There were still others—a little less deft with their attempts to make me feel any better—who pointed back to what they believed was my ill-fated decision to attend Harvard, rather than a school that would have better prepared me for a longer life in basketball, like North Carolina or UCLA. They had believed, at the time of my college decision, that I would regress in my abilities and lag in my development if I attended Harvard—where the level of competition on the basketball court was not nearly as high—and saw my release by the Atlanta Hawks, or any team for that matter, as inevitable and simply proving the correctness of their hypothesis.

Making matters worse, the regular NBA season had begun and the Hawks's first round pick John Brown was playing regularly and well, and would end up the season averaging over nine points per game that year. Accordingly, as folks were still learning of my failure to cross the expected threshold into professional basketball, his name would show up in the sports section of the newspaper in the box score as "J Brown," leading to awkward conversations around the neighborhood at the beginning.

"Hey, James. How are you back in town already? I saw that you had twelve points in Detroit against the Pistons last night—good game." And others, until everyone in the neighborhood eventually knew that the J Brown they knew wasn't the one in the box score for the Hawks.

After those two weeks of staying in the house, though, and through much honest introspection, the events and experiences of the last few years began to make sense to me. My time at Harvard and our team's inability to reach the expected levels of excellence and my failure to make it with the Atlanta Hawks of the NBA, and where and what the next steps for my life might look like, all began to become clearer to me. Some answers to what had occurred were painful to face and admit, as I continued to think through things in the midst of my self-imposed hiatus from the world. I think my parents knew that I needed that time, knew that I would eventually come to a better place.

The bottom line is that I didn't work as hard to *stay* on top as I did to get to the top. It was that simple. I knew all along from my time with Coach Wootten what it took to be successful. I was talented, but had always had to work diligently, and a little extra, to supplement my God-given talent, and to shape and improve it to the fullest. Most of us, even the Tiger Woodses, Peyton Mannings, and Michael Jordans of the world—are that way. There was sufficient talent at Harvard and in the Ivy League to challenge me to improve and to sharpen my skills, and the coaching staff was a solid staff, capable of teaching me all that I needed to know to continue to improve my game.

The skeptics may have thought right in predicting I would not enjoy athletic success at Harvard...that playing in the Ivy League would not prepare me for a career in professional basketball. The reasons for my failure were completely my fault, not Harvard's. I had spent all summer after the draft running, working, training, shooting, dribbling, doing everything I could to get ready for training camp. The reality is, though, that I had needed to do that for every summer of the four years I was at Harvard, not just the one summer before I was trying to step onto the stage of which I had always dreamed. Learning proficiency at a craft requires the steady, diligent application of one's focus and determination to that craft. Practice, practice, practice. The right way, every time. Time after time after time. Thinking that I could begin that kind of preparation at the tail end of my college career would not begin to make up for the lack of passion and determination that I had exhibited during my Harvard career. Obviously it didn't, and now I was in a nightmare of my own making. To some extent, I feel I also shortchanged Harvard University by not applying those things I knew I needed to do to improve during my time there. Maybe that's one of the reasons why our much touted recruiting class never lived up to the expectations which they, and others, had set for it.

All of this deliberation led to my initial conclusion that I simply hadn't been the self-starter in college that I had been in high school. No amount of looking outside for a scapegoat to pin the blame on would provide the answers I sought—Coach Fitzsimmons, the guy I was vying with for the twelfth spot, the level of competition at Harvard—none of those deserved that tag. Instead, and as hard as it was to face at that already difficult moment in my life, the answer to what had occurred was within me. I should have—and could have—put myself in a position so that anyone looking at and evaluating my basketball skills—even Coach Fitzsimmons— would see that my abilities were at such a high level they could not have even remotely conceived of cutting me. I had not done that, and therefore, when I looked in the mirror, I knew there was no one else to blame for what had occurred but me.

During this process of self-analysis, I also realized that my initial determination that I had been more self-motivated in high school wasn't *entirely* true, either. Rather, at DeMatha High I had the blessing and privilege of playing for one of the top high school coaches—ever—who built a great deal of his success on motivating his players to become more than they were at any given point in time. He had spent a career figuring out what buttons to push and levers to pull to get every kid to play as hard as he could, and getting them to practice and prepare year-round as well as he could. He didn't allow us to cram. Instead—in basketball and every-thing else we attempted to do—it became a way of life to continually work to improve. To use our God-given talents by making them even better. I couldn't take all the credit for my work ethic in high school—Coach Wootten deserved a lot of the credit, too. What I realized now—in this moment of failure—was that I needed to learn to apply those lessons on hard work myself, throughout my life. What would I do in the future with all the gifts and abilities I had been given, when given an opportunity to use and expand them—in whatever setting? I began to see it as a responsibility that I had as the recipient of those gifts and abilities—whether basketball related or otherwise—to maximize them to their fullest, for some purpose beyond myself. I was a steward of what had been given me. I was beginning to realize that I had not been a very good one up to this point.

I emerged from my bedroom renewed and with a fresh commitment to my future, and I vowed that I would never allow that to happen again in my life. Never again would I fail for a lack of preparation and effort over things that I could control. Never again would I fail to carry out the responsibility that was mine to make the most of what had been given me. That was a seminal moment in my life and career. I just didn't quite know yet how it would begin to flesh itself out in the days ahead.

A short time later, I found a job working, along with a teammate Floyd Lewis, within the District of Columbia government. Shortly thereafter, I went for an interview at IBM. Clifford Alexander, an alumnus of Harvard with whom I maintained a relationship, had followed my release from the Hawks and contacted me to tell me that he had arranged for an interview with IBM. Big Blue, with the very traditional corporate culture, including attire marked by white dress shirts and conservative clothing. I really hadn't paid attention to things like that before, worrying about how to dress for a particular environment, and I certainly hadn't done any homework before the interview to determine what a conservative company it is. I went over for my interview still in the mind-set of James Brown, ex-basketball player. I had an afro (I had been able to choose my own barber up in Cambridge, without Mom's input) and thick Clyde Frazier sideburns. I was wearing a velvet blue bow tie with a powder blue shirt, all crowned by a plaid blue suit and thick-soled checkerboard shoes. It seems I deserve some credit though, as at least I left the white leather coat with fur-lined hem and collar, and matching cap hanging in my closet as I prepared for the interview.

But did I mention that I was wearing a shoulder bag?

The man that I was to interview with came out of his office and began speaking with his assistant. I was the only other person in the reception area.

"Wow, James Brown, Harvard College, Harvard Speakers' Forum, captain of the basketball team, this is an impressive candidate. Where is he?" His assistant nodded in my direction.

"Here I is!" I announced, and leapt to my feet. (I didn't really say that, but I think that's the only way I could have made a *worse* first impression.) He brought me back into his office, sat behind his desk, and took time to instruct me.

"Son, if I didn't know that you were recommended by a Harvard alum of whom I think highly, I would have taken you through a perfunctory interview and bounced you out of here in a New York minute." I was puzzled.

"Why?" I asked.

"Why!?" His nostrils flared with exasperation. "Just look at yourself!" He then read me the riot act, informing me that my dress spoke volumes about me, and what I thought about this job opportunity, before I even opened my mouth, and that first impression alone indicated to him that I did not fit the IBM model. As a result, I now wear corporate dress when I'm in a corporate setting, down to making sure that my shoes are polished and my clothing pressed.

I didn't get that job.

As a result of that experience with IBM and the mentoring I received from the interviewer, things went better when I interviewed with Xerox—I began a job with them in sales, and eventually, sales management, in January of 1974. While I was there, my ultimate superior was Jay Nussbaum, a true marketing genius. I worked seven years at Xerox, learning a great deal from Jay, and building the foundation for much of my business career that was to follow.

After my first year there, however, I asked Jay for a leave of absence. Red Auerbach had popped back into my life again. Coach Auerbach had called and extended an invitation for me to participate in the Boston Celtics Training Camp for the 1974 season, to be held in Marshfield, Massachusetts. Jay was sympathetic to my request. He was a former athlete himself, having played football at the University of Maryland, and had hired a sales staff consisting of a number of former college athletes. His theory in hiring former athletes was his experience that most of those college athletes were competitive, self-motivating personalities and with those basic qualities they would be predisposed to success in the sales world. By and large I think he was right. Jay is one of the most inclusive executives I've ever seen, hiring minorities without a second thought. He was like my mom; skin color wasn't part of the criteria for his assessment of ability and potential. Jay has been remarkably successful his entire career, having been the global head of sales and marketing for a unit of Citigroup, the head of sales and marketing for KPMG Consulting, and the number three executive at Oracle under Larry Ellison, after he finished his tenure at Xerox.

Jay let me go to Marshfield, with a caveat.

"I think you need to ultimately answer the question in your own mind and either pursue it fully or get it out of your system, so I think it's important that you go." I nodded in agreement. I believed that I needed to follow this dream at least one more time, but would prefer that I did it without burning any bridges at Xerox. "What I don't want, however, is for this to be an annual event. Go this time and decide. See where it takes you, and determine where your lot lies. Basketball or business? Give it your best shot now, but I expect that you will not be coming back to me every year asking that you try out again."

I agreed. That seemed reasonable. And wise. I didn't want to look back when I was forty or fifty and wonder what could have been if I had tried to pursue my dream, but at the same time recognized that my departure, although temporary, would be disruptive to the company. I was going to make sure that there weren't any regrets this time.

The Celtics held their camp on an outdoor, concrete court. They were focused on finding out if you were tough and really a team player, willing to dive for loose balls knowing that you'd be skinned up as a result. I was willing and hit the court repeatedly during Celtics camp.

And once again, I was the last player released. Coach Auerbach sat down with me, and I'm sure he had a cigar somewhere that he was working on while we spoke.

"James, you've got what it takes to be successful in this league. You have the talent to make it in the NBA, but you didn't grow as a player in college. You've definitely got enough talent to play in the league; you just need to play against some top-flight competition to further season you." He wanted me to consider going overseas to play, to give me a chance to play regularly against better competition and sharpen my skills and get more experience under my belt.

The more I ruminated on it, however, the clearer my thoughts became. I realized that I wasn't interested in coming back and barely making a team. If I was going to play professional basketball, I wanted to at least be a seventh or eighth man, one of the guys that came off the bench regularly in each game. I didn't want to sidetrack my growing technology career to be a twelfth man, who played once a week for a few minutes, if that. I wanted to be a meaningful contributor to some team, some organization, whether that was in the NBA or on Jay Nussbaum's team at Xerox.

I decided that I had pursued the opportunity enough and had given it my best—despite having learned a lot about what my best would and should be in the future, but that it was time to continue to move on in a different direction with my life. I stayed focused on the tasks at hand at Xerox, and never looked back. Helping make my decision was the fact that the pay scales were similar. I was making as much at Xerox as I would have as a bottom guy on an NBA roster, which made my decision a little bit easier. I was on the path to somewhere in corporate America, I believed, and was now sure that I wouldn't be headed for a career in basketball.

About that time, I began my spiritual search by sampling a number of churches. Unfortunately, I wasn't being impacted beyond whatever I may have received in that hour. I still hadn't figured out exactly how to make my faith personal, and real. Obviously seeds were being planted, though, as I have a vivid recollection of driving home from a training session with Xerox about forty miles outside of DC, driving around in my little green Corvette. It was 1974, I was doing well, making great money at a huge company...but there was an emptiness that I felt. At that moment, for reasons I still don't understand, my soul was pricked. I realized that I had participated in the hedonistic pursuits of partying and engaging with others in regular happy hours, and hanging out at bars. I wasn't much of a drinker—I could only handle sweet drinks, things that tasted like Kool-Aid. But I realized that I hadn't been true to who I was, who my parents had raised me to be, and, most importantly, who God had created me to be.

And so, on a deserted road heading toward my apartment, I found myself beginning to pray. "God, I don't like this. I don't like who I am and what I'm doing. If You'll come into my life, I'll give my life to You and begin to follow You as best as I can." In that moment, I immediately felt as if a burden had been lifted from me, and felt a peace come over me, and emptiness filled.

Soon thereafter I was invited to a party and was hanging out with the guys, not doing anything awful, but behaving in a way that I felt was contrary to the commitment I had made on that deserted road to follow Christ—to make Him the Lord of my life. I felt like a traitor. I cried out again, asking for forgiveness and help. I left the party. For me, those series of events marked the beginning of my journey to follow Him as a committed believer.

Thereafter, I began to realize that my work ethic, doing the right things, my talent, education, skill, and whatever intelligence I had were only some of the elements of who I was and what I could bring to bear upon each day of my life to begin to live a successful life. I began to also see the importance of rising above the usual ways of climbing the corporate ladder that seemed to be at the expense of, or causing harm to, someone else. Seeing things that were done to climb the ladders of corporate success through the years made me vow that I would never do those things or take those shortcuts. I began to understand the difference between living a significant life, a life of real meaning that lifts others up, and a successful life, one too often defined by our society in terms of things and power and achievements.

I began to see co-workers not as competitors, but as allies and friends together in the midst of a cause greater than ourselves. I began to see the strains my superiors were under and as a result was able to do more to support their efforts so that they could be successful.

I began to accept more and more the responsibility for all I had been given. I began to be a better steward of all the gifts and opportunities that God had given me. I was beginning to build the foundations for the life that I was meant to live.

I began trying to find a church that would be the right place for me to worship. I bounced around for a while, but the odyssey ended when I attended and finally was planted at Rhema Christian Center Church. It's a Bible teaching church, and Clarence Givens, the bishop of the church when I arrived, provided the teaching of scripture for our congregation. It was almost like being in grad school for me, with the opportunity to dig deeply into God's Word, much like I had done with the various subjects in my classes at Harvard.

During my third year at Xerox, my father died. He developed pancreatic cancer in 1977 and died after a short illness at the age of 46. My sister had just graduated from Emerson College, and my father was so pleased that he was able to see her graduate. As president of the senior class, she spoke at the commencement and has always looked back with a warm gratitude that she had the opportunity to thank my parents from the podium, in public, for all the sacrifices they made to put her through school. At that moment, she spoke for all of us. One final thing: while in the hospital my father asked to be baptized. It made that day that he left us so much more bearable because we could take comfort in knowing that he is spending eternity in Heaven.

CHAPTER 6

THE FOUNDATION DETERMINES THE HEIGHT

Therefore whosoever heareth these sayings of mine, and doeth them, I will liken him unto a wise man, which built his house upon a rock.

Jesus, in Matthew 7:24 (KJV)

Everything that we want to have happen isn't going to necessarily happen, and if it does, it doesn't necessarily happen right away.

In the meantime, build the foundation.

I certainly found it to be true in basketball, both in my successes and my shortcomings. The times when I had laid a proper and solid foundation, I was able to achieve more of what I had set out to achieve. When I tried a shortcut around laying a proper foundation of fundamentals, I wasn't able to reach the same heights. I was also discovering the same in my faith; going deeper in Christ must come before we can grow higher with Christ.

Depth before height.

I heard a sermon on that topic when I was working at FOX Sports in Los Angeles. It was a powerful sermon delivered by Bishop Charles Blake of West Angeles Church of God in Christ. I realized that's what Coach Wootten had been talking about for all of those years, just in a different lexicon. That's what happened to me in college—I hadn't spent the time to prepare my basketball foundation sufficiently to support me as I tried to move on to play at the NBA level. As I tried to go higher, the support—the foundations—simply weren't there to achieve the career that had been the focus of my dreams. Once the foundation is set, whatever it is, the ultimate destination, the ultimate height—more or less—is determined. It won't go any higher or further than whatever the foundation will support. The superstructure you are attempting to build is determined by that portion that you can't see—that underground foundation.

Let me be very clear right now, before we go any further, as to what I mean by "depth" and "height." "Depth," of course refers to the foundation we build or need to build that will undergird everything in our lives. That foundation includes our faith, our character, integrity, and honesty, living a life marked by humility and stewardship—recognizing that everything we have comes from our Creator and everything we are is the way He created us.

Our foundation reflects a proper understanding of, and a committed focus to, the most important priorities in our life—faith, family, and friends.

The depth in our lives—the strength of our foundations—is marked by courage. The courage not only to pick yourself up when you fail or fall and move on, but to step out, anxiously at times, from your comfort zones. And probably most importantly, to embrace the courage that causes you to continually look at yourself in the mirror—to see who you are—and to change what you need to change.

As to "height," let me tell you first what I don't mean. Height has nothing to do with trophies, résumés, and awards. It is not a scholarship to Harvard University. Height has nothing to do with the amount of money you make, the number of cars you have, the house you live in, or the size of your investment portfolio. It has nothing to do with positions or titles or the number of people you supervise. Those are all the measurements of a society that ascribes success to climbing ladders, and in terms of the acquisition of things, achievements, and power.

Some of those things may occur along the way, but they are not the objective of what I mean by "height."

Instead, "height" is very simply striving to become all you were created to be. It involves maximizing your God-given gifts and abilities, finding those things you are passionate about and pursuing them, recognizing the opportunities you have each day to add value to the lives around you, and to make a difference in your world. It is demonstrated in the number of times you picked yourself up after you failed or fell. It is reflected in a life that recognizes the platforms for positive influence you have been given and the opportunities we each have as role models to change just one life.

Height is also reflected in a life that sees everyone as someone special. That is something I keep foremost in my mind—to remember to treat everyone as someone special—because they are. Everyone has a gift, a talent. Everyone has something valuable to contribute to the whole, to the team.

The foundation determines the height—and the impact you will leave in this world. That will determine the level of success in your life, regardless of the final verdict imposed by the measurement of success by society.

I was trying to build upon that solid foundation of my trust in God for my growing faith. Actually, my sister Alicia and my mom played significant roles in building that foundation. Alicia was the first in our household to accept Christ, which she did during her sophomore year in college. Her real growth spiritually occurred a couple of years later, when she began to take more time in reading her Bible on her own, and in attending a weekly Christian Fellowship group on Thursday nights, instead of merely going to church once a week.

My mother had grown up in a Baptist household, with ministers throughout the family. Sometime after Alicia had graduated from college and moved back to DC, her influence led Mom to accept Christ as well. This was a wake-up call for the rest of us, because this meant that Mom realized that despite her background and our upbringing on Godly principles that something was missing in her life. Despite the Godly example she had always been throughout our childhood years, that all-important element of a personal relationship with Jesus Christ was missing.

As I later learned myself, she was right. We had a "head knowledge," in that we grasped the Bible and its stories intellectually. What we didn't have was a "heart knowledge," in that we had yet to ask Jesus to come into our hearts and to accept Him into our lives.

As the Apostle Paul wrote, "Dear brothers and sisters, when I was with you I couldn't talk to you as I would to spiritual people. I had to talk as though you belonged to this world or as though you were infants in the Christian life. I had to feed you with milk, not with solid food, because you weren't ready for anything stronger" (1 Cor. 3:1–2a NLT). Most of us start as new believers at a younger age, and then learn and grow. Mom started her personal relationship as an adult. When she accepted Christ into her heart, she already had such a vast knowledge of the Bible to fall back on, a knowledge that was now infused with a spirit on fire to learn more about God and walk even more closely with Him.

She matured very quickly in her faith, and then Alicia and Mom turned their attention toward me. They were concerned about me and my salvation, and with those two set on that course, it was inevitable—just a matter of time— before the same result occurred in my life.

*   *   *

I realized somewhere along the way in the building of my foundation of faith that true success comes from the Lord. I know that may seem trite to say—we've heard it so often, even maybe misused at times. But I have learned that to be a truth in my own life. While we are charged with working as diligently as we can—my vow to not fail because of a lack of preparation—any worldly success we have is truly just an undeserved blessing from God, whether or not we acknowledge it at the time. The circumstances of each day, over which we have no control, are too varied and numerous for any of us to be able to anticipate or control for our good. He will pave the way, He is our advocate. "For promotion *cometh* neither from the east, nor from the west, nor from the south. But God *is* the judge: he putteth down one, and setteth up another" (Psalm 75:6–7 KJV). I have clung to this verse for years. I understand it to mean that I do not need to blow my own horn.

There has become something of an epidemic of self-aggrandizement, self-promotion in our world. Popular self-help books on business speak of promoting your accomplishments; other people have public relations firms on retainer, and so on. I'm not saying that there is anything inherently wrong with those things, but rather that promoting ourselves shouldn't be our primary focus. We live in a "Look at me!" world, but I think, instead, we should rely on a foundation that is first and foremost built on a relationship with God. He can and will do the promoting for us, and bring others along in the process to help—therefore, be appropriately modest.

God gave you special gifts, to be sure, but He also gifted everyone else in some form or fashion like no one else. So while you are unique and special, remember that everyone else is as well. Build on the foundation of those gifts and abilities He has given you. Become all He created you to be, and leave the promotion to Him and others He brings alongside you and into your life.

When I was at Xerox, in 1974, a member of the senior management team, Addison Barry Rand, a truly gifted executive, outlined certain principles for success to a number of us on the company's sales team. Over the years I have refined his list, embraced it as a continuing part of my personal foundation building, and have had the opportunity to share it with numerous and varied groups, and to young people in particular. It's merely a call to remember the fundamentals of life, or for some young people—who are where I once was—a chance to hear, learn, and internalize what I believe are the essential fundamentals for success in their lives.

I refer to them as the Ingredients for Successful Living, but they consist of what I believe are my seven fundamentals for success. Rather straightforward and easily made a part of your daily living, the seven ingredients consist of Good Communication Skills, Appearance, Personal Relations,

Punctuality, Thirst for Knowledge, Being a Team Player, and Overcoming Adversity.

As for the first, Good Communication Skills, this includes not only speaking and writing, but maybe most importantly listening. *How* you speak and *what* you say, matters. Jesus said, "A good man out of the good treasure of his heart bringeth forth that which is good; and an evil man out of the evil treasure of his heart bringeth forth that which is evil: for of the abundance of the heart his mouth speaketh" (Luke 6:45 KJV). Time and again, the Bible cautions us on what we say, pointing out that it is reflective of our thoughts and our inner being. As the book of James notes, both salt water and fresh cannot flow from the same spring. Your speech has the power to inflame and hurt. You can wound those around you.

Many times the best thing you can do is to be quiet, and listen, as your speech can even show your ignorance. While it's always good to remember the cautionary words attributed to Abraham Lincoln, that "'Tis better to be silent and be thought a fool, than to speak and remove all doubt," there's another reason to be silent. Those that you meet can provide significant learning opportunities for you. Don't be afraid to stand on the shoulders of giants, as I have had opportunities to do. Those that have gone before me have learned things that they can share, and often will, if I simply ask. And I can't learn if I'm so busy speaking through what they have to offer.

I was guilty of this early on in my career when I was in local government, while making a sales call early in my career. I had arrived late to travel to the appointment with a co-worker, to call on a person that I had known growing up. I was comfortable in my previous relationship with them—too comfortable—and slipped into colloquial speak, the language I would have used around the neighborhood, not in business. I didn't realize until later that I was being disrespectful, to both my co-worker and the person we came to see.

The co-worker traveling with me that day was Bill Curry, one of the senior salespeople and one of the top salespeople in the country, year after year. He was also black, and he spoke with me afterward.

"One, don't ever be late again for an appointment that we're going on together. I won't tolerate that. I deal with these people in a professional light and I want to be viewed in that light. Two, you treat these people with respect. They are in a business setting and have earned the title and position that they enjoy, and you should treat them that way."

I learned another reason for listening that day—you send a message to the person that they have value, that they are someone special, that what they have to share is important to you, and that getting to know who they are is more important to you than telling them who you are.

The second ingredient, Appearance, I learned in that office that day at IBM when I interviewed right out of school. The way you look matters—clean and neat, properly dressed, shoes shined—and makes a very clear statement about you, and what you think of the situation and the people in front of you, before you even open your mouth. This may seem a bit superficial but remember, our objective being to become all we were created to be and making a real difference in the world, acknowledging some things of the world, if they don't compromise core foundational beliefs, is necessary.

There was another occasion, early in my business career that showed that my IBM experience hadn't fully taken hold yet. The athletic world has always viewed dress as more avant-garde. It's a little more on the edge. Accordingly, I went on a sales call with a female co-worker, and dressed as if I were still in college. Looking back, I realize I must have looked more like someone she had picked up off the sidewalk as she was walking into the building than a co-worker as she and I went to a sales call at, of course, a more staid and subdued corporate environment. I was wearing a black dress shirt, a black suit with a "pattern" of red splatters, a red tie and pocket square, and red leather shoes. I was an absolute mess, but I sure thought that I was the epitome of style. Looking back, I'm grateful for how patient people were with me in those days as I was learning how to build the foundation.

I'm not suggesting with this ingredient, or with any of these, that you conform, but do understand this: there are acceptable dress codes in life at times. Absolutely true. At the same time, we have far too many people today who are willing to conform, to change who they are to please their peers or to fit into society in some other way. There is a more fundamental way. Be true to yourself. My faith also speaks to this point, as the Apostle Paul wrote to the believers in Rome, "And be not conformed to this world: but be ye transformed by the renewing of your mind, that ye may prove what *is* that good, and acceptable, and perfect, will of God" (Rom. 12:2 KJV).

Do not be conformed to this world, but don't be so caught up in individuality for individuality's sake that you put yourself at a disadvantage. Remember that your ultimate goal—the "height" you are headed for—should be to become all you can be using the gifts and abilities you have been given. You can't do that locked in your room, or by staying in your office—you have to walk in the world. There is a level of acceptability and credibility you need to have in the world to be taken seriously. Look, my outfit before the Harvard/BU matchup was because I liked a very trendy style of dress back then and thought the look was cool. There was not anything inherently reflecting who I really was substantively in the look. Don't unthinkingly conform on issues of substance. But don't limit your options and opportunities to make a difference and to become all you can be—unnecessarily.

I love Josh Hamilton's story. He was the first overall selection by the Tampa Bay Devil Rays in the 1999 amateur baseball draft. Over the next few years, he fell prey to the demons of substance abuse, an issue that afflicts countless numbers in our nation, and Josh was completely out of baseball for nearly four years. The Rays, understandably, moved on without him. During those dark days, he had twenty-six different tattoos etched on his body, including one of the Devil on his left arm.

Hamilton's story, however, doesn't end with those lost days. He has been clean and free of drugs since October 6,

2005, crediting his personal saving relationship with Christ for the transformation. Major League Baseball tests him three times a week, which helps him with his accountability. But the tattoos remain, reminding him of those dark days. And so he is back playing baseball as one of the best players in the game, living up to his potential, covering his tattoos with clothing.

You may change your mind someday about how you want to look, but the piercings or tattoos you get in the meantime to "express yourself" to feel part of a group you really don't want to be part of for the long term, or to claim some other identity to feel accepted, may be permanent. Or someone else may have different ideas about them—totally unrelated to your reasons for them in the first place—or your clothing, and make a judgment about you in the interim.

For me, I wouldn't close any doors unnecessarily. I now dress conservatively, figuring that I should err on the side of conservative attire. That's the world in which I walk. That's the world in which God has me at the moment where I can make a difference. I can always dress in a way that more reflects me when I'm with people that already know the content of my character.

If you make a decision that you want to be in a certain kind of arena, then study the culture of that arena, the kind of "uniform" that they wear, and get on board with it. If everybody who works there wears purple shorts and that's what it takes to get in the game, and you want to be a part of that game, then I suggest you get purple shorts—and wear them. If you don't, then make a decision to go elsewhere, or create your own institution with your own attire. But if you do stay the course and pursue the purple shorts position, don't be upset if they decide to hire someone else, anyway.

Just understand that most people will interpret you based on how you look and are attired. It's often the first thing they see, and the first impression they have. Maybe it shouldn't be that way, but I can tell you that it most assuredly is. You told them with your attire that you weren't interested in understanding the mores of their group. You subconsciously, or intentionally, have given them a glimpse into your heart as it perceives who they and their organization are.

The heart is the seat of who you are and your outward appearance and actions reflect to the outside world what is in your heart. It is where God looks, also. He is very clear about that. When the Lord was directing Samuel in his search for the next King of Israel, Samuel kept bringing Him the most handsome, well-built, bright men in the kingdom—all of David's brothers. God kept refusing, and finally said to Samuel, "Look not on his countenance, or on the height of his stature; because I have refused him: for *the* LORD *seeth* not as man seeth; for man looketh on the outward appearance, but the LORD looketh on the heart" (1 Sam. 16:7 KJV). And the smallest brother of the lot—David—was selected, because of his heart.

However, most people stop at the outside and don't look at the heart often enough. For better or worse—probably worse—they look at outward appearances. And they end up by doing that too often, to judge the person—and who they are and the state of their heart—by their appearance. Fair? Not always. Reality? Most always. Therefore, don't handicap your journey to reach your goals and make the difference you dream of making, whether through chances in business, in relationships, or in other venues before you have the chance to make a statement and impression of who you are—in your heart. And when you yourself move into a similar decision-making capacity, like those you found yourself before, remember this conversation we've had so that perhaps you take a longer look into the heart of the person before you, rather than at their outward appearance.

Third, your Personal Relations skills are important to building the foundation. Some refer to these as interpersonal skills or an emotional intelligence quotient. How do you relate to others? Can you support those around you? Can you be trusted by those around you? The answers must be yes. You have to have the character and integrity to be trusted by those around you—those who depend on you, and on whom you also depend.

I had the privilege a number of years ago to host a panel of high-level corporate leaders, including former President George H. W. Bush, Tony Robbins, and General Norman Schwarzkopf, Jr., on a television program called the "Corporate Leadership Speakers Series." General Schwarzkopf made an observation during the program that I have not forgotten. He noted that an examination of failures at the highest level in corporate America—those at the "C-level" (CEO, CFO, COO, etc.)—indicate that the overwhelming majority are failures of integrity. The last few years are

replete with examples of companies that have either suffered significant losses, or gone completely out of business,
reducing shareholder value and destroying their employees'
pensions along the way, because of a failure of integrity at
the top.

These Personal Relations skills—the ability to get along
with and support others—are predicated on a realization that
we live and work in a glorious mosaic, this United States of
America. People are not all going to look like you or speak
like you. They will have vastly different backgrounds and
childhoods that will impact how they see the world. People
from different cultures and genders bring different talents
to the table than you bring, and gifts that we all can benefit
from. To treat them and those gifts in any way other than as
sacred is not only not right, but is not the best way toward a
successful life—a life that realizes we live in a world of people
from different cultures, backgrounds, life experiences, and
beliefs. Being able to connect and interact with others different from us—without compromising our core beliefs—is
crucial to our ability to work effectively in a diverse world
and have the fullest positive impact we were meant to have.

I love the biblical truth, "every joint supplies."[1] Para-
phrasing Ephesians 4:15b–16, we are all a part of the body
of Christ with a specific role to play. Every single joint in the
body meets a unique need and is no less—or more—important
than any other members of the body. We see this firsthand
every day on the athletic fields and courts. Teams, which I'll
talk a bit more about in the context of another ingredient,
comprise wildly different members, and the best-performing

ones, those high-impact teams, are the ones that draw on the talents of each and every one of their members.

Fourth is Punctuality. Being prompt makes a statement about you, and, like your appearance, usually does so before you even have a chance to open your mouth. It shows reliability and dependability, and maybe most importantly, it shows that you respect those who are relying on you and that you respect their time.

To be perfectly open and honest, this is the area that I struggle with the most. I've discovered that there will always be things in our lives to improve, and for me, thus far, this has been the most difficult to remedy. I have learned to call well in advance, when I realize that I'm not going to make it somewhere on time. That's not preferable to making it in a timely manner, of course, but I think it is a reasonable and responsible antidote. Don't just show up late. At best, you'll have shown yourself to be undependable; at worst, you'll be fired, or not have a chance to develop further the relationship, or do further business with those you left dangling while you were late. None of those results are anything that you want. I worked with a great salesman at Xerox who was terrific at his job, and was making six figures a year back in the late 1970s, yet was fired. He was habitually late, and couldn't be relied upon, and, finally, that mattered more than his ability to generate sales commissions.

Fifth, you need a Thirst for Knowledge. This is more than simply intelligence, but rather a desire to keep learning and improving. Never think of yourself as having arrived, but rather, realize that you can become an expert in your position, and to do so you will need to remain open and look to keep learning. Continuing education will help you grow, and will help you in what should be your quest to becoming the best and most valuable resource that your team or business enjoys.

Despite my presence in the broadcasting world for a number of years, recently I decided to try and improve in my profession. A number of other broadcasters have visited with linguists or diction coaches, and so I decided to attend a speech workshop with Dr. Teresa Nance, Assistant Vice President of Multicultural Affairs, at Villanova University, in the not-too-distant past. I never want to assume that my diction is as precise as I hope that it might be—I'm always concerned that mispronouncing a word could lead to someone interpreting that as a lack of professionalism or intelligence (remember, ingredient one on Good Communication Skills and the inferences people will draw!).

And so there I was, sending a videotape for linguistic analysis by Dr. Nance. Doctors and lawyers take continuing education courses, soldiers continue to train, and I'm always going to work to speak as clearly and region-neutrally as possible. We can all be open to improving our skills. And I thought it went pretty well, to be honest.

I arrived in Philadelphia to meet with her and learned that I didn't enunciate anything longer than a one-syllable word properly. Once she was done working with me—despite the fact that she worked to help me with those words—I still went through a several week period during which I was hesitant to do anything but grunt. However, through the experience I learned a number of exercises to warm up my voice that I still use that have helped me continue to improve. Or at least I hope they've helped me improve... or I may go back to the monosyllabic grunting.

Ingredient six: Being a Team Player. This deals with how well you function within a unit, and whether you can be a contributing part of that. Humility is a component of this—does it all have to be about you, or can you redirect praise and support others, even when you may not get credit?

People tend to use the word "team" to describe any group of people working together. The reality, though, when you look closely at them, is that they may be nothing more than "a group of people working together." Those in the group are only focused on what *they* are doing, apathetic to others in the group and how they could help them to do what they have to do. It is all about doing their individual jobs. Tension and conflict tends to set in, meetings get longer, disagreements get more personal and in the end their efforts often fall short of the mark.

Successful teams, on the other hand, have a clear mission or purpose for existing—a clear objective and direction in which they are headed. Every member of the team—if it is to be a successful team, i.e., one that achieves its objectives—has bought into the mission. They believe in it and are passionate about it. They understand it and know where they are going and with whom they are going. They know who the leader is and have allowed and enabled that person to lead the team by their individual and collective commitment and cooperation.

Successful teams are characterized by members with different skills, abilities, and life experiences that when meshed together for the sake of the mission—which they believe in—result in successful outcomes and high impact for their organizations. Within such teams, each member of the team recognizes and values the different gifts, abilities, and life experiences that each team member brings to the cause. A successful baseball team wouldn't put nine first-basemen on the field at the nine different positions around the field and expect to be successful. A team that will be successful and have a meaningful impact within their organization, within the community or beyond, is one where each member of the team recognizes the value each member brings and realizes that without each member their chances of being successful—fulfilling their mission—diminish.

Being a team player requires that basic understanding of the makeup and functioning of successful teams. It requires an understanding of how your individual and interdependent role, along with the other members of the team, contributes to the success of that team. It is a high calling—where not only is your value to the effort recognized and applauded by the others, but where everyone on the team puts the welfare and success of the team and its mission first and foremost. Teams comprised of members like that—team players—achieve not just good results but extraordinary results. It is critically important to "check your ego at the door" when preparing to engage in a team-oriented activity. It is amazing how much can get done when no one is concerned about who gets the credit. Red Auerbach always wanted to get "inside the statistics" of a winning effort: who deflected a pass at a critical juncture in the game, whose harassing defense upset the other team's rhythm and so on, because as he knew, the maxim "a rising tide lifts all ships" is true.

Sometimes, actually, I should say regularly, if my experience is anything like yours, we will be confronted by challenges in life. It's not a question of whether they will occur, but when. That leads to the final ingredient, Overcoming Adversity.

Trials and tribulations will come into every life. That's reality. That's promised by the Bible. It doesn't say that they *might* come, or that we *may* face them. The Bible says that these times *will* come for all of us. The good news is that through these challenges, our character is revealed and given an opportunity through which to grow.

The Apostle Paul reminds us of that when he says, "And we rejoice in the hope of the glory of God. Not only so, but we also rejoice in our sufferings, because we know that suffering produces perseverance; perseverance, character; and character, hope" (Rom. 5:2b–4 NIV). And James encourages us to "consider it pure joy, my brothers, whenever you face trials of many kinds, because you know that the testing of your faith develops perseverance," and follows by noting, "Blessed is the man who perseveres under trial, because when he has stood the test, he will receive the crown of life that God has promised to those who love him" (James 1:2–3, 12 NIV).

Therefore, when these trials and tribulations come, what

is your foundation built upon? Hopefully it's on bedrock, and not sand. And if you have a tried and true set of philosophies (or for me, my faith) that you can rely upon, then when those times come, you will be able to stand fast.

Working in and around the NFL as I do, every year we see examples of teams that face adversity. Everyone suffers injuries, or draft picks don't pan out, or times when they just aren't playing well. Those teams that stay the course and stick with their solid foundational principles always seem to be more successful—over the long haul—than those that frequently change coordinators or head coaches or playing styles. It's no accident that the Pittsburgh Steelers have had one ownership family and only three head coaches in the last thirty years, and lead the NFL with six Super Bowl championships. The Indianapolis Colts and New England Patriots of the last few years have shown similar adherence to consistency.

In addition to the seven Ingredients for Success, I also believe that there is one underlying thread of these fundamentals—competence to do the job at hand. At Xerox, that meant that I had to have the ability to actually make sales. I had to be able to meet my monthly quota. However, even with the ability to do that, many fall far short of the levels they might rise to professionally because of their inability or unwillingness to comport their behavior to the objective criteria. Without that fundamental level of competence, it's unrealistic to think about promotion and rising to greater responsibility if you can't handle the current level of responsibility you've been given.

And if you've got these core foundations, there is no reason that you can't have fun along the way. This is not a dress rehearsal; your life is happening, now. And you can enjoy it. Make time to do so.

———— ∞ ————

My concluding thought on this is my most important.

I don't think it's possible to reach one's highest potential without a life rooted in Christ.

Applying these ingredients will lead to success, absolutely, for the principles are true. Even those who don't believe or are not people of faith can apply these and achieve worldly success. However, I have come to believe, that my potential—your potential—as the human being who God created, won't ever be fully realized without God within you and walking with you. The role, or roles, I was meant to fulfill in my lifetime can never be achieved to their fullest without a relationship rooted in Christ. I may accomplish great things in the eyes of the world, but in the eyes of the only One who matters, I will have fallen short without Him in my life helping and guiding me in the role I was meant to play in my journey.

Having said that, let me be very clear and very open and honest with you—I'm not where He wants me yet. I don't know that I will ever be. My personal relationship and walk with Christ—starting in my late 20's—has been a journey of learning, reaching, and continually falling short. I have, on too many occasions, fallen off the right path only to have to pick myself up—or perhaps it was Him picking me up—and get back on the path to try again. I have made mistakes along the way that I should not have made—and as to which in my quieter moments I knew better. The last thing I am suggesting is that I am some kind of expert on a life rooted in Christ and what it should look like. I'm not.

I've made some good decisions in my life too—and I'm sure He was smiling down on me for making them at the time. But I've made a lot of mistakes, a lot of wrong decisions. Things which did not honor Him.

My hope is that you will take something away from my sharing of some of those mistakes in my life, the heartache and turmoil they caused, and the struggles to get back on the better path He calls me to—as well as from some of the things I've done right. If that occurs and helps you in your journey through life, I will be blessed and humbled.

There is a scene in the Old Testament book of Joshua that I love. Moses, the great leader of the Israelites has just died, having never reached the Promised Land. And now we find Joshua, standing on the banks of the Jordan River as God's next annointed leader.

Three times God tells him to be strong and courageous (see Joshua 1:6,7, 9) and also gives him the recipe for the rest of his journey and that of God's people whom Joshua has been appointed to lead.

In Joshua 1:8, God states, "This book of the law shall not depart out of thy mouth; but thou shalt meditate therein day and night, that thou mayest observe to do according to all that is written therein: for then thou shalt make thy way prosperous, and then thou shalt have *good success* [emphasis added]" (KJV).

Good success. I had always thought success was simply success, but upon seeing this emphasis, I realized that there are different types of success.[2]

God's success is "good success." It's significance. It's making a difference in the lives of others. It's Joshua standing on the banks of the Jordan River, feeling anxious and inadequate, and realizing that he is being called to do something that will make a difference in the lives of the people he is being called to lead. And in that moment, it's Joshua also realizing that he can only do it with the leadership and in the strength of God. We all will have our moments where we face our "Jordan River" as Joshua did. But like Joshua, under the leadership and with the strength of God, we too can cross it, and find that in the journey under His guidance we will make a significant difference in the lives of those all around us.

When you and I live a life that strives to make a difference in the lives around us, realizing and confessing that we can only do it under the leadership and in the power of God, then we begin to live that life that will be marked by "good success"—a life of significance.

And I suspect that you will find that your sleep at night will become more peaceful and restful, knowing that you are doing what you are supposed to do—the right thing, the right way—by living a life that honors God.

As I admitted, I haven't always been there, but in our home now we claim another verse from the book of Joshua, if for no other reason than to remind me not only of the right way, but also of some of the wrong ways of my life.

Joshua, later in his life, says it clearly, when he says, "Choose you this day whom ye will serve...but as for me and my house, we will serve the LORD" (Joshua 24:15 KJV).

It all starts with the foundation. Build it wisely and well.

CHAPTER 7

JOINING THE NETWORK

*The most important thing to remember is this:
To be ready at any moment to give up what
you are for what you might become.*

W.E.B. Du Bois

About five years into my tenure with Xerox, I got an opportunity to work in broadcasting doing work as a commentator for the formerly named Washington Bullets, now the Washington Wizards. Petey Greene, a DC broadcasting legend who overcame his criminal past to carve out a space on the airwaves, opened the door for me. Petey, whose story was the basis for the movie *Talk to Me* with Don Cheadle in 2007, paved the way for my entry into television by having me on his local television show. Having gone through the attempt of trying to make it in professional sports, Petey wanted me to speak to his viewers about failed dreams, and how you can pick up the pieces and make a successful transition in the journey of your life. Something about my time with him in that segment must have impressed him, because he told me of an opening in the sports department at the station. The color analyst was stepping down, and he thought I should audition for the position. I wasn't sure that I knew enough to even sit for the interview, let alone get the job, but Petey demanded that I go. I agreed.

In college I had played against the Bullets' star player at the time, Phil Chenier, and Phil agreed to come to my audition with me during his day off. My goal in bringing Phil, a tactic I had picked up in my years with Xerox, was to show that even if I didn't have experience, I was aware enough to bring the team's star with me to simulate a halftime postgame interview. For my audition, I simulated a halftime interview, which no doubt went better than it might have, given my pre-existing comfort level with Phil. I called on help from Coach Wootten, who agreed to call the general manager of the Washington Bullets, and whose son went to DeMatha, to vouch for my work ethic. I was pulling out all the stops, and being known as a District of Columbia high school basketball star didn't hurt and, I suspect, also contributed to my getting the job.

Through that experience, I got the broadcasting bug. It was a blast, and the money—well, it was hard to top the allure of $250 per game! It truly was a labor of love, which was more important than the money. My co-workers at

Xerox thought I was absolutely insane. Here I was, giving up my vacation time so that I could travel with the team and work both home and road games for the Bullets.

I covered about twenty-six Bullets games that year, and the next year continued with those games, while adding a few games for a fledgling network in the area, Black Entertainment Television (now simply BET). They were producing tape-delayed games of historically black colleges, and those, along with the Bullets games, continued to add to my growing broadcast experience. During this time I was still working full time for Xerox, and using my vacation time for broadcasting. I added some regional games for TVS, founded by network pioneer Eddie Einhorn, who later became the head of CBS Sports and is now a co-owner of the Chicago White Sox.

Over a relatively short period of time, my experiences kept expanding. I worked some track and field events for USA Network, simply adding to the Bullets, BET, and TVS broadcasts, while always looking to add other opportunities. I was really enjoying it, and at the same time was starting to toy with the idea that I might like to transition into broadcasting full time. If I was ever going to do that, I needed to continue to work hard and garner more experience and contacts—I was not going to let anyone else out there with the same dream outwork me.

At some point during this journey, I began to pray for clarity. I was twenty-eight, and prayed that God would give me some clarity as to my career path during the next five years. I'm not entirely certain how I decided upon that time frame, but I knew that it wouldn't happen overnight, and knew that I would need to keep laying a foundation for whichever direction I ended up traveling. And I didn't want to moonlight for too long, and potentially negatively impact my business career. I figured that making a decision by the age of thirty-three would leave ample time for that career path I was meant to travel—whatever it turned out to be.

During that time, I had a momentous experience. I was walking with the Bullets players from their locker room after a loss toward the team bus and saw a young boy fall in beside one of the star players. He asked for an autograph—not the best timing, I could see. The player brushed the piece of paper aside with the back of his hand, acting as if he didn't see him. The young man started to walk off, when Wes Unseld, truly the Bullets best player and later an NBA Hall of Famer, who had been trailing the young man and thereby saw the entire encounter, picked up a huge assist in my book.

"Hey, can you come over here for a minute?" he called. The young man paused and followed, as Unseld introduced himself and sat the young boy on his knee. Unseld spoke with him about life for a few minutes, while the other players undoubtedly watched from the bus, which was delayed from departing. I could see the Bullets trainer readying the bus to depart, but I knew that he would never give the word to leave as long as the Bullets team captain was sitting outside. Unseld gave the boy an autograph and a hug, and the young fellow, whose shoulders were slumped just minutes before, stood straighter before my eyes that evening, as he walked off into the depths of the stadium, his confidence restored.

It was a great example of the truism that we all are role models, and all can positively impact someone, if we just take the time to do so. Whatever our sphere of influence—NBA Hall of Famer, neighbor, parent, or co-worker.

I was not the only person moonlighting from Xerox; others were as well, but they weren't doing it in such an open and highly visible way. My immediate supervisor kept tabs not only on what I was doing at Xerox, but also on all the other jobs I was covering as well. I think he resented the other things I was doing, and I think he resented that Jay Nussbaum was helping facilitate my second career—Jay's only caveat being that I still had to make my sales numbers with Xerox, which was not only reasonable, but appropriate. I had to continue to meet or exceed my expected numbers, and I always did. But for some reason, my supervisor at Xerox at the time began to make life more difficult for me in the office. As a result I ended up leaving Xerox in 1979, after spending almost seven years with the company, and took a job with Eastman Kodak.

I worked around eighteen months for Kodak, and was confronted at that time with a dilemma. They wanted me to move to their corporate headquarters in Rochester, New York. Leaving the Washington area would put a significant crimp, if not end altogether, my fledgling broadcasting career. Instead, I accepted an offer to join a minority-owned software development firm, Raven Systems, where I spent the next year.

I continued to moonlight with TVS and the other networks, as well as doing some occasional freelance work for Channel 9, the CBS affiliate. I received a call from Marty Aronoff, the sports producer at Channel 9, at two in the afternoon one day, while I was sitting at my desk in my office. Up until that point I had done fill-in work, like public affairs segments on weekends. This day, however, Aronoff informed me that the regular sportscaster, the wildly popular Glenn Brenner, was ill, and the weekend sports anchor, longtime Washington Redskins voice Frank Herzog, was out of town. They were in a bind, so they called me to see if I would do the sports segment on the six o'clock news broadcast. They must not have realized just how desperate that made them seem. I had never done it once—weekend or late night or even for practice—never. And so I hurriedly agreed to do it and hung up, before they realized what they were asking.

I arrived and Aronoff told me that he would type my script for me. "What you'll do," he said, "is to read the script that we've got for you, and when you get to the asterisks in the script, look down at the monitor on your desk. There you will see the highlights that are playing for the viewers." I had it, I assured him.

I took my place on the set, but was so nervous and cotton mouthed I could barely speak when the anchor tried to transition to me. I had no idea how to gracefully segue into the piece, so I merely started running through the script, and when I hit the asterisks, I looked down and began voicing over the highlights, as instructed. I was great. I was really getting animated: "The Bullets played the Knicks last night, and here you'll see a long jumper from—"

Mom's Notable Quotes

<u>Wisdom and Encouragement:</u>
"If God says so, no man can say no."
God will make room for your talent."
"God will redeem the time."
"Better to have and not need, than to need and not have."
"I don't trust man for anything, but God for everything."
"God will make a more excellent way."

<u>Every Sunday after church:</u>
"Go wash your hands, before you come in the kitchen."

My father and I after a radio interview with Voice of America, I did as a high school senior. Boy, those pants were made to order, huh?

Mom receiving an achievement award as a department manager for a leading local store.

High school graduate photo. DeMatha Catholic H.S. in Hyattsville, MD. Class Vice-President, 1969.

College graduation photo. Harvard University, 1973. Seated next to me is my sister Alicia, and mom is next to her. The Walt "Clyde" Frazier influence is evident with the facial hair. Oh Boy!

Harvard Basketball
photo, early '70s.

On a cruise with my daughter...don't run away dear, daddy knows
how to do hair!

Left to right: Me, Dorothy, and Pastor Givens.

Fun night out. Los Angeles, CA. Left to right: Fred Johnson, Demetria Johnson, Dorothy, and myself.

My wife and I. Is that smile a thing of beauty, or what?

A very happy milestone for the Brown Family. Katrina's wedding day. Left to right: Father of the bride, stepmom Dorothy Brown, mother Alfreda Holmes, Katrina and John Walker.

Dancing with my baby.

Christmas photo of my son-in-law John, my daughter Katrina, and my grand daughter Kaela...they went to purchase shoes right after this photo was taken!

Yours truly hugging my wife Dorothy. Seated are my great aunt Ozie Powell and her daughter Carolyn at their home in Hattiesburg, MS. Aunt Ozie is one of the most saintly Christians I've ever met.

It was always a special occasion when we had my mom over to our house…and my in-laws wanted to be there to enjoy her company. Left to right: My wife Dorothy, me, mom, and my father and mother-in-law; Leroy and Auguste Johnson.

The five siblings standing in front of my home where we celebrated Mom's 70th birthday. It was a grand time, and an emotional one. Left to right: me, my brother Everett, sister Alicia, brother John and brother Terence. Background: my brother-in-law Fred Johnson.

My mother, Mary Ann, giving me instructions at her birthday celebration. I affectionately referred to her as the "Sergeant." There was no debating her orders! And I'm a better man for that.

Pre-show photo with *Tonight Show* host Jay Leno, flanked by my wife Dorothy (left) and daughter Katrina (right).

Climbing Mt. Kilimanjaro, as an assignment for CBS Sports. You can tell I'm *thrilled* with the couple days worth of climbing we've already endured. The mountain's height is 19,340 feet.

A slimmer me working at the 1992 Winter Olympics in Lillehammer, Norway. Three Norwegians who could've played on ANY NFL offensive line!

My high school coach Morgan Wootten, and I co-hosting popular high school basketball program on local TV station.

The legendary Arnold "Red" Auerbach and the ever-present victory cigar.

A cherished photo with one of the legends in sports broadcasting history, Jim McKay at his ranch in Maryland. Radio producer Bruce Cornblatt on the right.

I mentioned to the valet at the hotel I was there to interview Kobe Bryant and the attendant wanted to park my car in the lobby!

Post-radio interview photo with the man who was the inspiration behind my desire to attend an Ivy League school. Former Princeton and New York Knicks great, ex-Senator and presidential candidate, Bill Bradley.

The NFL's greatest wide receiver, Jerry Rice of the San Francisco Forty-Niners. He made sure to protect his hands with gloves, even when just shaking hands!

Philadelphia Eagles QB
Donovan McNabb and
I after a pre-game show
interview.

A hug from my
daughter Katrina
always brings out
the biggest, radiant
smile for me.
Credit: Anita Bartlett

Larry Fitzgerald, premier wide receiver with the Arizona Cardinals, and I
share a good laugh at the NFL PLAYERS Gala upon his receipt of the 2009
JB Award for Impact. Credit: Donald Miralle for NFL PLAYERS

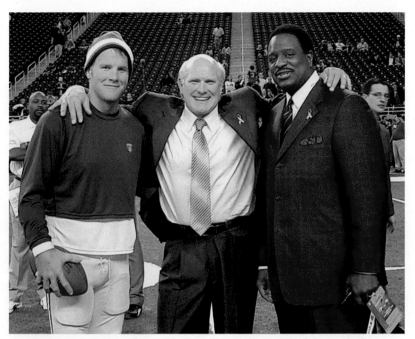
Former Green Bay Packers QB Brett Favre, Terry Bradshaw, and I.

The *FOX NFL SUNDAY* crew. Left to right: Jimmy Johnson, Terry Bradshaw, me, and Howie Long.

Bill Cowher, me, Cris Collinsworth, and Phil Simms during one of many light moments on the set of the Emmy Award winning *INSIDE THE NFL* on Showtime.

The CBS crew of *THE NFL TODAY*. From Left to right: Shannon Sharpe, Dan Marino, me, Bill Cowher, and Boomer Esiason.

I glanced over at the monitor to see the highlights, and all I could see was the top of my head. I slowed my reading…and stopped. I looked up toward the camera. As it turns out, they'd had a tape malfunction and here I was, still on camera, with no videotaped highlights being played for the viewers. Just my face. And so, I smiled.

"Hi, there," I said into the camera. I had nothing else. Somehow, I stammered through the rest of the broadcast, and actually reached the point where I had run *over* my segment time. They were giving me the cut sign. For those of you keeping score, that makes both "what to do when the highlight tape malfunctions" and "this is what the cut sign looks like" as two things they did not cover with me before the broadcast. I had no idea what they were doing with their now increasingly frantic hand signals, and just kept speaking into the camera.

The producer finally whispered to the camera operator, who began turning the camera away from me and back to the anchor. All I knew was that I hadn't finished the piece, and with the camera turning away for some unknown reason, I began climbing over the desk to stay in the picture.

I was awful and should have, by rights, been fired on the spot. Instead, for some reason, somebody saw something worth redeeming in me.

I was still doing the color commentary for the Bullets alongside Frank Herzog. Frank was also working at Channel 9, at the time when I was doing some freelance work there, and in 1981 he left to join the ABC affiliate, and asked me to come over as his weekend anchor and weekday reporter at Channel 7. These were dizzying times for me. So much was happening in my personal life and career, and I was wrestling with what to do about the offer. It seemed like the answer I had been seeking in my prayers, but I was still reluctant to leave the business setting that had been so good to me already.

I sought out Mike Trainer for input. Mike was an attorney who was the manager of Sugar Ray Leonard at the time. I told Mike of my concerns in leaving the business world for broadcasting, which at the time seemed to be such a tenuous existence. Mike took a fatherly tone with me, and hit me right between the eyes with his very frank advice.

"It sounds to me that what you're looking for is a guarantee in life. You're looking for an absolute safety net, that if it doesn't work out in broadcasting, you've got a place to land. It doesn't work that way; that's not life."

He paused to make sure that I was grasping it all.

"You're only as good as your ability to perform or create value and have an asset that others see as being valuable. *You've got to get out of that scholarship frame of mind.*"

I was trying to be methodical and deliberate in my decision-making process but sometimes there comes a point when you have to embrace risk and your dreams.

I accepted the position and adopted a free-agent mentality in evaluating all my offers from that time forward. After I made the move to a career of full-time broadcasting, someone at CBS saw me doing a college basketball game for TVS, which was regionally syndicated on NBC. Because CBS had just acquired the rights to March Madness, the NCAA

Men's Basketball Tournament, they were looking for additional announcers to use for the first weekend of games in the spring of 1982. I was blessed that Ted Shaker, an executive producer at CBS, liked my work, and they added me to do more than just the four games of that opening round, and I was able to broadcast some NBA games for them.

While I was at the ABC affiliate, Channel 7, I asked repeatedly about a contract. Upon hiring, they had offered me a contract, and despite Mike Trainer's advice, I still wanted whatever guarantee in my new life that I could get. No contract. Months went by, and they continued to offer to get me one, but could never deliver it. As a result of my working as the weekend reporter, and college basketball analyst for CBS as well as some NBA games, my exposure within CBS was increasing. I was concerned about working for the dual networks, and didn't want it to negatively impact me down the line, so I kept asking for that contract from the ABC affiliate. For whatever reason—maybe they weren't sure that I was going to pan out—they never provided one.

After six months, the CBS affiliate at Channel 9 offered me a full-time position. They were going to create a sports segment on the five o'clock news show and wanted me to be on it. My agent was thrilled, and pointed out that it would probably be in my best interests to be with the CBS affiliate, since I was wearing the CBS jacket to broadcast NCAA and NBA basketball games on weekends. We figured a time was coming when ABC might not like that arrangement. Still, I wanted to talk with the local ABC affiliate to see if they were going to give me a contract and had any further thoughts on my future with them.

I enjoyed the people and the management, but was unclear as to their long-term plans for me. As my agent pointed out, it was their failure to give me a contract, despite months on the job, which was even giving me the opportunity to go to CBS.

"Can't I at least go speak to ABC?" I asked. "No," he advised. He thought I should take the CBS deal without alerting ABC to the possibility. I ended up taking his advice, and that ended up being a tumultuous time for me. It didn't feel like that was the right way to go about it, and I should have followed my instincts on that. Things were not as clear as I had hoped in trying to access what was before me. The only thing that seemed clear was confusion. I sought a clear voice, and a clear direction—but none seemed to come. I realized though, later, that my instincts may have been the voice I was searching for in the chaos. Channel 7 had never given me the contract they had promised when I had repeatedly asked them for a mutual commitment that we could enter into, but even with that my instincts pointed me toward what I knew to be the right thing to do. To talk to them. I didn't follow those instincts and as a result things got messy.

Not surprisingly, as soon as Channel 7 got wind of my impending departure, they immediately pulled me off the air. Everything happened too quickly, before I even had a chance to speak with management at the station who had given me my first full-time position. Sometime later, I was with the owner of Channel 7, Joseph Albritton, and had a chance to explain what had happened and to apologize. As I anticipated, he was gracious about my departure, despite how poorly I had engineered it. I was grateful, because although that was the right move, it was the wrong way for me to have handled it, and I didn't want to have burned any bridges in the industry.

In 1984 I began working with CBS full time, broadcasting on a daily basis as well as doing a sports anthology show on the weekend *CBS Sports Spectacular*, where I covered everything from rock climbing to, eventually, the Tour DuPont bicycle race.

Through it all, I have had a desire to press ahead and learn from life and its ups and downs, and that has caused me to add Psalm 91 to my daily prayers. Every morning I go through a list of prayers, many of them prayers of supplication, asking for help and protection over those I know personally or know about. However, much of my prayer time is focused on the condition of my heart, and whether I am seeking God with all of it. Psalm 91 is, to me, a prayer for comfort and deliverance, and a reminder that God is with us at all times—in the good and not so good moments of our lives.

> He who dwells in the shelter of the Most High will
>   rest in the shadow of the Almighty.
> I will say of the LORD, "He is my refuge and my for-
>   tress, my God, in whom I trust."
> Surely he will save you from the fowler's snare and
>   from the deadly pestilence.
> He will cover you with his feathers, and under his
>   wings you will find refuge; his faithfulness will
>   be your shield and rampart.

You will not fear the terror of night, nor the arrow
that flies by day, nor the pestilence that stalks
in the darkness, nor the plague that destroys at
midday.

A thousand may fall at your side, ten thousand at
your right hand, but it will not come near you.

You will only observe with your eyes and see the
punishment of the wicked.

If you make the Most High your dwelling—even the
LORD, who is my refuge—then no harm will befall
you, no disaster will come near your tent.

For he will command his angels concerning you to
guard you in all your ways; they will lift you up in
their hands, so that you will not strike your foot
against a stone.

You will tread upon the lion and the cobra; you will
trample the great lion and the serpent.

"Because he loves me," says the LORD, "I will rescue
him; I will protect him, for he acknowledges my
name.

He will call upon me, and I will answer him; I will be
with him in trouble, I will deliver him and honor
him.

With long life will I satisfy him and show him my
salvation."

(Psalm 91 NIV)

And to that, I can only say, "Thank you." He has certainly
delivered me through the challenges and chaos of career

changes, the responsibilities and challenges of fatherhood, and the many trials of my life thus far.

Through all of that, He watched over me as I stumbled, then picked me up and sent me out into another day.

And tomorrow is another day.

CHAPTER 8

LESSONS FROM ALBERTVILLE

I have a dream that my four little children will one day live in a nation where they will not be judged by the color of their skin but by the content of their character. I have a dream today.

Martin Luther King, Jr.

I was now at Channel 9, the CBS affiliate in DC, and was still doing extra games and other assignments as they came up for CBS, as well as broadcasting games for TVS. I stayed there for about two years as I recall, when CBS, the parent company, made me an offer to join their sports network. With that, I came on board as a full-time analyst, doing college and NBA basketball games, as well as various anthology shows. Hubie Brown was the A-team analyst, while I was the B-team analyst.

After a short period of time, Executive Producer Ted Shaker took me aside to tell me that although my work was great, with my lack of big-time athletic credentials, my best hope for longevity with them and in this business was more than likely as a play-by-play announcer, not an analyst. There would always be star players retiring, or fired coaches looking for work, all of whom would have greater name recognition with the public with the real possibility of pushing me out of a job every year. If, however, I became a talented play-by-play announcer or a studio anchor, my future could be brighter, more secure, and longer. Since Shaker was the one who gave me the opportunity to expand my role at CBS, I took his advice to heart.

I applied myself diligently to both endeavors—commentator or analyst and play-by-play announcer. Some time thereafter, I had an opportunity to do the play-by-play broadcast for a game in the National Football League.

My first NFL game was, well, to put it bluntly, not my finest hour. I had spent a great deal of time boning up on football—after all, I was a basketball guy. Ted Shaker and Senior Producer Ed Goren took the time to fully brief me on all of the guidelines that would help me with the broadcast: take my time, use the clock in the booth not the stadium clock, relax, and so forth. The Atlanta Falcons were playing in Tampa, and both the Buccaneers and Falcons were not expected to do well that year. While the rest of the nation was probably watching Philadelphia, Dallas, or San Francisco, our game was being broadcast into very few homes—hence the reason why I was chosen to do it—and probably had a viewing audience consisting only of "a couple of houses in Tampa and the TV trucks at the stadium," we joked. And even the folks in those houses and the TV trucks probably wished they were watching the Eagles, Cowboys, or 49ers instead.

However, after the first half I got to feeling my oats, thinking that these play-by-play duties weren't all that difficult. I had settled into the role. It wasn't a surprise—the way I approach things, my preparation had been laborious, and it was paying off in aces. In fact, I got so comfortable, that midway through the third quarter, I heard myself say, "It's third down with seven yards to go for the Buccaneers. They come to the line with two backs in the backfield. Steve Deberg takes the snap and hands off to James Wilder. Wilder hits a big hole off-tackle! He's at the thirty-five, the forty! He's at the forty-five, the fifty, the fifty-five! And he's finally brought down at the sixty-yard line!"

The producer shrieked into my headset from his place in the TV trucks outside: "THERE IS NO SIXTY-YARD LINE! Go to commercial!"

Flustered, I looked to the stadium clock for the time, so that I could make the transition to commercial and save the little bit of any dignity that still remained. "And so, it's first and ten for the Bucs at the thirty-five of Atlanta, and with eight minutes and *ninety-nine seconds* left in the third quarter, we're going to take a station break." I was in a downward spiral, so rattled I couldn't even read the game clock, or at least remember that it would go above fifty-nine seconds.

Not only did they not fire me, but I bounced back well enough from that debacle with my continuing work, because after a period of time I was asked if I would prefer to be the main studio host for the NCAA Men's Basketball Tournament Show, or the lead play-by-play announcer for college basketball. Being a team player, I indicated that either position would be a dream come true, and I was honored that I was being considered. I would let them sort it out based on their needs. I did tell them that my preference would be to become the lead play-by-play announcer, but that really I would be just as pleased with the other role.

I was then asked, "And, of course, you would be the first African-American lead play-by-play announcer of a major sport at a network. How would you handle that?" I was startled. I hadn't seen that question coming, or realized that my race still mattered here in the late 1980s.

"Hopefully with the same degree of excellence that I've handled my body of work that has led you in approaching me with this opportunity."

I got neither job. They selected Jim Nantz, a good friend of mine and a superb announcer, as the play-by-play announcer for college basketball, and Pat O'Brien as the studio host for the NCAA Men's Basketball Tournament Show.

I got the news that I had been passed over for both opportunities and was crushed. When I regrouped from that setback I found myself on the verge of giving serious consideration to leaving the business. I figured that if I couldn't move ahead in that sport—college basketball—that I had actually *played* and therefore knew best, what were the chances that I would get an opportunity in anything else? Again, the path I had assumed was clearly mine to follow—wasn't.

My partner in the broadcast booth, Dan Jiggets, who happened to be a former Harvard football player, incidentally, made it very clear to me that I couldn't quit. Dan and I made up the first all-black NFL broadcast team that did a full season's worth of games, and had overlapped in our attendance at Harvard. Dan now provided the counsel that would resonate with me in a way I remember thinking of earlier in my playing days, but had relegated to the back burners of my thoughts.

"James, you can't quit. You have pushed the line for so many young people who will follow, that you can't step out now. You have to press on."

I remembered when I was playing at DeMatha and then attended Harvard, the thoughts which inspired me to push myself even harder back then, that I wanted other kids in the neighborhood to feel that they too could reach and achieve things they dreamed of doing. Maybe this was more than just about me. Dan's words struck home and stuck with me.

My loved ones got involved too. My sister was instrumental in strengthening me to respond appropriately to that disappointment, reminding me to continue to work at the things within my control. I just had to remember, and be patient in the knowledge, that God would do what He will do with me, in whatever place, and in whatever time He saw fit. "In the fullness of time," she said, "God will open whatever doors He wants opened for you."

She then turned the analysis back toward me. Was there anything else that I could be doing to improve and sharpen, she wondered, any skills that would help me in the future? With that in mind, she sent me to work with a speech therapist (the same one I mentioned earlier) to polish up my diction. My wife, Dorothy, who was my girlfriend at the time, reminded me that promotion does not come from ourselves, as stated in Psalms 75:6–7, but from God. My mother told me to take heart that God would make room for my talent and to just hang in there. Boy, all the women in my life!

I continued to be a sideline reporter at CBS, and to work as diligently as I could and have faith that God was already in my future. For me, I was confused and uncertain in the present. Not only was God with me at that moment, but He already knew what my future held.

Sure enough, it wasn't long before a door opened.

I was selected to be the host of an early afternoon show covering the XVI Olympic Winter Games to be held in Albertville, France, in 1992. Armed with that upcoming assignment, I experienced the games and learned firsthand all I would need to know about their broadcast production.

While there, I found myself at dinner with a producer from another division at the network one evening. He may have had too much to drink, because all of a sudden he seemed much more open and candid than he may have wanted to be, which he probably realized when the light of the next morning broke through his window.

He leaned in closer to me at one point. "You know, your colleague at CBS Sports would make an excellent Olympics prime-time host, not only because he's a super talent, but because he doesn't look like he's black." Then he realized what he said and *to whom* he said it.

I just stared at him and didn't say a word. It was 1992 and I was hearing this from an educated, top network producer. I was amazed and I'm sure the look on my face must have betrayed both my amazement and shock. Yes, my own birth certificate read "Colored" under Race, but I would not think that a producer I barely knew would share what he was obviously thinking in his heart—underscoring in my mind, how much further we have yet to go in matters of race.

His comments confirmed in me my belief that an emphasis on understanding and embracing diversity, and the benefits realized from that kind of enlightenment, must remain as an important aim of our society. It is important for at least two reasons: one, as we saw during the presidential campaign of 2008, that even though we have made tremendous progress, race and gender were still negatively injected into the discussions and two, that I'm sadly suspicious that it stems from the simple fact that still not enough people are comfortable in diverse company, nor do they recognize excellence comes in more than one color.

We've come a long way, but we still have a ways to go.

At the core of any continuing progress we will achieve, though, is the need for rational, civil, frank, respectful communication. The creation of moments and pockets of opportunities by and between neighbors, educators, politicians, sports figures, businesses, Realtors, parents, students, and others that allow for a dialogue about our apparent differences, understanding that despite our disagreements and differences we are still here together for better or for worse, will lead to a future that we would all like to claim to be better than where we were yesterday or are today.

One of the things that is both so simple, and yet so difficult, for many is to comprehend the power of apology. We see it in our daily lives, and in particular our interpersonal relationships. I can't stand it when there is a misunderstanding between myself and my wife, and even more so when it comes about as a result of my actions or words. Many times, I'm ashamed to say, she beats me to the punch, and, without regard to who is actually at fault (usually me), she will apologize. "Honey, I'm sorry for the role I played in creating this misunderstanding. I love you very much. Will you forgive me?" Of course, it makes me feel like an incredibly small person since I know good and well that I was the one who caused the problem. But that's the power of apology and forgiveness, and the truth, that we're all given the ministry of reconciliation.

That's the power of communication.

At the same time, someone who has been dealt an injustice can extend forgiveness, even when no apology is given. It doesn't have to be expressed but can simply be engendered by a change of our hearts. To carry bitterness or a sense of having been wronged within us only holds us back from becoming all we were created to be.

It is a choice each one of us has to make for ourselves—but it is our choice. Why choose to be bitter the rest of your life? We were each created by God with unique gifts and abilities—like no one else. No one. If we don't use what we have been given—who will? Who knows what good could have been done, and who knows what the world would have missed, or could have looked like, while we sit on the sidelines playing a role as a victim. So, why not use those gifts and abilities? We are given the ability to overcome obstacles in this country with all of its opportunities, and by a God who created us, loves us, and walks with us. It won't always be easy, but with God's help, we can overcome hardships...and—in His strength—learn to forgive. Even if that forgiveness doesn't come about from someone who has done something wrong who should be asking for forgiveness or extending an apology.

On December 1, 1955, in Montgomery, Alabama, a lady named Rosa Parks refused to move to the back of a public municipal bus. That's all. She refused to give up her seat in the front to a white man as a local ordinance required. She didn't hit anyone. She didn't curse at anyone. She just didn't move. And as a result, she was arrested. Her arrest led to a year-long non-violent bus boycott in Montgomery which eventually led to a change of the ordinance.

Those who attempted to march peacefully on March 7, 1965, from Selma to Montgomery—and were stopped six blocks into the march at the Edmund Pettis Bridge by mounted police wielding billy clubs, tear gas, rubber tubes—had a dream. They refused to be relegated to the life they were in, for themselves and for their children and grandchildren to follow. When I think about some of the challenges I've faced, and to some degree still encounter, I often think about how those who've gone before me dealt with barriers, indignities, and life-threatening situations. But also, how some who were witnessing a wrong were willing to "step up to the plate."

Branch Rickey, president and general manager of the Brooklyn Dodgers, was one of those willing to walk alongside others to help them to become all they can be. In 1945, Rickey signed Jackie Robinson to play in the Dodgers baseball organization, and on April 15, 1947, Jackie Robinson became the first black man to play baseball in the Major Leagues.

He played that year and throughout his career for the Brooklyn Dodgers. That year he was named the National League's Rookie of the Year. Two years later, in 1949, he won the National League batting championship with a .342 average and was selected as the National League's Most Valuable Player. He ended his career with a lifetime .311 batting average and in 1962 was elected to the Major League Baseball Hall of Fame.

But Jackie Robinson's life and career were not all glory and awards. Instead it was one in which he was constantly faced with painful racial slurs and hatred from people with unfounded and deep-seated prejudice toward blacks in general, simply because of the color of their skin.

And, as the story goes, on one occasion more than two generations ago, when Jackie Robinson's team was playing in another city, angry racial taunts aimed at Jackie Robinson continued during the game with a deafening force. A white teammate, Pee Wee Reese, the shortstop and a much respected captain of the Dodgers called time out right during the middle of the game. As the crowd began to quiet, wondering what was unfolding before them, Reese slowly walked over to Jackie Robinson, put his arm around his shoulder, and stood there silently.

It was a wordless, but eloquently powerful message which said to the now silent crowd: This man is my friend. This man is my brother.

And I would add—a wonderful child of God.

Jackie Robinson knew breaking the color barrier in the Major Leagues of baseball would not be easy. But when given a chance—he got up and lived the life he was meant to live, while others came along beside to walk with him, and he made a difference for those who would follow.

There are hundreds of stories like theirs.

I have one of my own from an early age. In elementary school I checked out a book from the library: *So You Want to Be a Doctor.* Upon seeing it, a teacher of mine took it upon herself to let me know—and she had to realize the adverse impact this would have on me—that because "kids like me" weren't good in math and science, I didn't need to worry about being a doctor. If she did think she was doing me a favor, it seems like a poor way of inspiring children to dream and reach for the stars to me. Unfortunately for me, it took me longer to overcome the blow to my self-esteem than it did for my friend Dr. Ben Carson, who is probably the preeminent pediatric neurosurgeon in the world, despite overcoming many obstacles along the way. Although I'm not a doctor, I am now fully aware of the power I possess through either words of criticism or "healing words." A quote by Richard Parsons, the former Chairman and Chief Executive Officer of Time Warner, has served to encourage me. As best as I recall it, he said that he refused to let someone else's narrow-minded perception of him limit him in his pursuits. That still serves to encourage me.

Martin Luther King, Jr., of course comes to mind. Non-violently walking where he knew he would have to walk.

There have been people of all races, gender, and others standing behind other artificial barriers society erects to keep people apart, who have refused to be left out. They didn't pretend as though the system worked or that society was just—instead they pushed on and through to make their lives better. Believing by doing so, that they would also make it better for others. They refused to allow their situation to define who they were, who they could be, or who they were meant to be.

They were people of all races, cultures and ethnic origins, gender and age, men and women, girls and boys, from all walks of life and diverse backgrounds. Past and present heroes, who followed their dreams, rose above their circumstances and refused to allow themselves to be relegated to a victim mentality, though many had every right to feel that way. They didn't always succeed the first time or the second time. Sometimes they didn't seem to succeed at all—at least by the standards of society. But in God's eyes and by God's standards for success they were successful by trying to overcome the obstacles before them and picking themselves up over and over when they fell or failed.

It's time again for all of us—no matter where we find ourselves this day—to follow the example of those heroes who went before us, and become, in God's eyes, the successes He created us to be.

And as you step out in that journey, you've got to understand the obstacles before you and always be willing to learn from your mistakes. Once you've accomplished that, all that remains is a positive attitude, "I will attempt to do whatever it takes to overcome whatever might be set up against me—to believe that it is possible for me to go where I should go." A defeatist attitude won't do anything for you except be the actual cause of what holds you down.

And these messages we hear that if you're poor, or black the only avenues open to you are through sports or music—these messages serve to further propagate the lies of the voices that want to create a picture of a limited range of opportunities. I didn't come from a wealthy, connected background. Many of my friends did not, either. Something like seventy percent of the millionaires in the United States are first generation, meaning that they didn't come from a wealthy background. They figured it out themselves, using education and persistence, as my parents taught me, along with God's favor, to rise above their beginnings. As has been said before, it's not where you start, it's where you finish.

But don't think that I'm talking about money; it's about others. If you are promoting others above yourself, these things will take care of themselves. If you are giving someone a good, solid, day's work, if you treat others with respect, if you give to others and help to lift them up with you, if you treat everyone as someone special, then you will begin having good days. When you give, you better prepare yourself to receive.

The Bible states that He will open up the windows of Heaven and pour you out an ongoing blessing that will be more than you can even receive. It may be contrary to what the world believes, but it's true—I have had firsthand experience of His blessings.

What I need to improve on in particular is how I multiply those blessings. How do I multiply those blessings I have received from the lives of others? And the best way I know of to do that is to walk with and alongside someone who needs you—and add value to their life.

My mother's father was able to rise above his humble beginnings as well as overt racism that existed at the time. As I described before, this remarkable businessman in Hattiesburg, Mississippi, had the first black-owned dry cleaners, a hugely popular nightclub and restaurant—and a baseball team. I thought that was so cool. He came from an era in which he had to stay in separate hotels, and travel by separate (and allegedly equal!) means, but he was bound and determined that he would overcome.

The landscape of our country has witnessed a great deal of improvement over the course of my lifetime, such that we recently saw an African-American elected president of the

United States. Regardless of where you stand politically, I think it is encouraging to see the support that he received across racial lines, and most encouragingly, by young people who didn't see color in a stereotypical way. Of course, they grew up in a different era than others.

Similarly, this has been an encouraging time as well with respect to gender. At the same time, note though, how many people told pollsters during the campaign—usually off the record—that they were not going to vote for a black man, or a woman.

The eleven o'clock Sunday morning hour has been referred to as one of the most segregated hours in America today. The sad irony is that many Christians, I believe, are some of the most sympathetic people to racial issues and the struggle for justice and acceptance across all lines of diversity that tend to separate us. However, I see very encouraging signs and strides that we will, hopefully, continue to grow past that with interracial congregations and denominations. The Promise Keepers movement created an environment for many Christian leaders to come forth and together address deep-seated hurts and biases, both conscious and subconscious, and move toward reconciliation and growth.

At DeMatha High School we were a close-knit basketball team, and it was a unique experience, especially against the backdrop of the 1960s. We were all impacted by Coach Wootten and that environment, however. One of my teammates at DeMatha was Kerry Scanlon, a white player. Kerry is now a partner at a major law firm in DC, and while at

DeMatha really took his role to improve the racial environment to heart.

Kerry's family had moved from northern Virginia to Maryland for the sole purpose of allowing Kerry to play for Coach Wootten at DeMatha. Kerry played for Coach for only his senior year, the only player to have done that, and during that year, he became very close to me and the rest of his teammates. Kerry said that he had never really thought about issues of race before, having come from an all-white school, but now with a number of black teammates at DeMatha, he suddenly had to think about it.

He transitioned beautifully into our team, thank God, hanging out with us, spending nights at our homes, and going to parties where he was the only white in attendance. We became roommates the following year when we arrived at Harvard. Kerry played basketball in college as well, and also took an interest in other pursuits, one of which was his growing interest in civil rights. After he finished at Harvard, he attended law school, and has worked in the Civil Rights Division of the United States Department of Justice, as well as with the NAACP. He credits his interracial experience at DeMatha with placing him on the path he is on, trying to seek and provide justice for all.

As a broadcaster, I am ever vigilant to be mindful of the power of words and the positive impact they can have on broadening what too often has been a myopic viewpoint about color, and moving toward one in which people are judged only by the content of their character. Early in my time with CBS, Ted Shaker, the network producer, conducted a seminar to make sure that we were being conscious of the words and phrases we used, as well as reminding us that we have a responsibility as announcers to be fair and balanced in how we announce a game, and to be mindful of the stereotypes and biases that we may have. He pointed out that many colloquialisms and expressions are rooted in insensitive mindsets, and carelessly chosen words.

One example given during the seminar was of a video clip of Larry Bird, a white player, making a play that was described by the announcers working the game at the time in terms of "smart," "savvy," and "heads-up." They spoke of the thought process behind the play and how quickly he processed the play as it unfolded.

They then showed a highlight of Magic Johnson, a black player, making the same play, and his play was characterized by the announcers in physical terms, in terms of "strength," "agility," and "athleticism." It was instructive for all of us, because many of us announcing can fall into those same thought patterns as well, and continue to perpetuate an unfortunate stereotype.

One of the participants with me in the seminar was Tommy Heinsohn, the former Celtics great. Tommy and I had a wonderfully open and honest conversation afterward, as Tommy admitted that he didn't understand the big deal that was being made of the announcers' descriptors. "Help me understand, JB. That was an amazingly athletic play that

Magic Johnson made. Incredible body control. Why is that bad to say that?"

"It's not," I told him. "You're absolutely right, except that you—or anyone—has to be even in their treatment of the two players. If calling it 'athletically amazing' is a compliment, then why would you shortchange Larry Bird when making the same play by simply saying he was 'smart'? Wouldn't he also want—and deserve—to be called 'amazingly athletic'?"

Tommy, to his credit, understood it. And my time with Tommy is characteristic of what I would hope we could all accomplish if we sat down together and talked. Openly, civilly, respectfully, wanting to understand, and without anger.

There is power in that kind of communication. Bridge-building power.

There is nothing wrong with recognizing and celebrating our differences. We all have different gifts—every joint supplies. But we need to make certain that we're celebrating them—not differentiating between each other—because of them.

We still have a ways to go. We've come a long way for sure. And together we will get there for a better tomorrow.

CHAPTER 9

MY DOROTHY

A wife of noble character who can find?
She is worth far more than rubies.

Proverbs 31:10 (NIV)

I met Dorothy Johnson when I was working at Channel 9, shortly after my poorly handled move from Channel 7. I was a longtime bachelor, often dating, but not very seriously, and certainly set in my bachelor ways. One of the reasons that I was slow to get serious was that I wanted my daughter from a previous relationship, Katrina, to be involved in the process. And I was very comfortable in my bachelor role, at least for then.

Therefore, we took it slowly, Dorothy and I. At the time we met, I had what I felt was a crush on someone else, a co-worker at the local CBS affiliate in Washington, DC. I went down to her floor to ask her out, and she made me aware that she was engaged to be married to one of the marketing executives, another friend of mine. That bit of news ended the crush. However, she did tell me that she and her fiancé had a friend that I just *had* to meet.

Great.

I'd been down the whole "you've got to meet my friend" route before, so I didn't show much interest. I told them that if we could work it out sometime, that would be great. I'd be happy to meet her. We tried to double-date a few times, but the timing never worked out. Finally, they invited me to their wedding that summer, saying that their friend, Dorothy, would be home from college and would be there and I could meet her in the midst of the other people who would be attending their wedding, without any pressure on either of us. I agreed, but actually skipped the wedding—I didn't want to look like I wanted to get married—and headed, instead, straight to the reception. The wedding party was late in making their appearance—I waited about two hours at the reception with the other guests—and so I eventually left without meeting her.

Dorothy and I chatted several times by phone when she was back in school at Hunter College in New York City. We were discussing what would be a mutually convenient time to try and finally meet. That would happen on Thanksgiving weekend, when Dorothy would be home in northern Virginia for the holidays. She agreed to meet me at the TV station after the late newscast. When I got word she had arrived at the station, I sent one of the sports department interns down to the lobby to greet her and to give me an advance scouting report. He came back just as I was going on the air, but gave me a two-thumbs-up, and I raced through the news that night to get out of the studio and meet her. That evening, I discovered that not only was she very pretty, but more importantly, she was a very nice lady and I found myself enjoying her company. I found out she had been born in Kitzingen, in what was then West Germany, when her father was stationed there in the U.S. Army, and from there the family moved to Fort Meade, Maryland, when she was thirteen.

From the outset of our budding relationship, we tried to be realistic about the physical distance between us—she was in New York in school, while I was in DC. That distance could make things more difficult than they might otherwise be, but we both thought it was worth giving it a try. We agreed that if things got too difficult, or if one of us wanted to see other people, that we would just be straightforward about our feelings and let the other person know.

And so sometime not too long thereafter, she fired me. That's what I called it, anyway. She was very kind when she called, but said that it was just too difficult to date long distance. It just wasn't going to work. Thankfully, a short time later, she called me back. She realized the error of her earlier decision, and our relationship was back on.

The fact that I was working college basketball games for CBS Sports had me traveling to New York City fairly frequently, helping our relationship tremendously. At one point in our long-distance journey together, Dorothy was in

Virginia visiting with her parents and decided to cook for me one evening. She was preparing goulash. That first dish she prepared for me really underscored how much I wanted the relationship. She was very proud of her goulash dish, and I of course couldn't wait to try it. It was horrendous. I plastered the biggest possible grin on my face that I could muster, and told her it was great. I even asked for seconds. That didn't bode well for our future together, however, as I was so spoiled by my mother that I hadn't learned how to cook, either. If this relationship was going to continue to get serious, something had to change, if for no other reason than our mutual survival.

Over time our relationship became more serious and reached a point where I felt I was finally ready to propose to Dorothy. However, I knew I needed to talk to Katrina about it first. Katrina had spent a great deal of time with Dorothy during the times Dorothy and I had spent together in DC. I told her of my decision, and as we talked, she asked me if she said that she didn't want me to marry Dorothy, whether it would make my difference in my decision. As it turned out, she was jerking my chain, and said, "How could somebody not like Dorothy? Of course I'd love for you to marry Dorothy."

And so, after we had been together for several years of dating, we became engaged. There wasn't much change until another several years passed, and we finally set a date— January 1, 1994. That's when the tension really began to set in, at least for me. I had been a bachelor for so long that I was starting to sweat bullets with the prospects of all of that changing. I was having second thoughts—that had nothing to do with Dorothy. She was wonderful. It was me. I didn't know anything else but my bachelor lifestyle. Of course, that lifestyle was all about—me. I had no one else to worry about in my personal life—but me—and of course, my daughter. Decisions regarding what I wanted to do or places I wanted to go—were about me. I was seeing the end of all of that, and I'm sorry to have to admit, I wasn't sure I could, or wanted to, give it up.

As the date drew closer, there were so many "voices in my head" about what this commitment meant, comprehending what this lifestyle would entail and the like: bottom line is, I got cold feet. My way of dealing with it was absolutely a coward's way. While in Los Angeles on assignment I called Dorothy on the telephone a week before the wedding and said to her that I love you, but I couldn't go through with the wedding.

Dorothy was as composed as ever, and very clear in her response that was along the lines of, "James, I appreciate your honesty, and you have to do what you feel in your heart. But, will you kindly do me a favor, please don't ever call me again." I said okay. From that point forward, for the next few weeks, I don't remember a thing. Time stood still. It's all blank.

I was not in a good place.

I was lethargic for weeks thereafter. Three months later, I was still in terrible shape. I missed Dorothy to the point of hurting deep in my soul. I was an emotional wreck when I discussed how I was feeling with one of the ministers in our church, Tony Jefferson, telling him that I had made a dreadful mistake. He already knew *everyone* at church knew and all were certain that I had made a dreadful mistake, including my mother and the rest of my family. (In fact, I wouldn't be surprised to learn that they were secretly plotting to get Dorothy into the family and me *out*, if I hadn't come to my senses.)

Dorothy and I had each spoken with our pastor Clarence Givens separately, and he was excellent at giving each of us counsel based on the Word of God. He did not take sides or point fingers of blame, but rather gave us each a chance to speak with him and share what was in our hearts. I still have a vivid recollection of him looking at me when I finished and saying, "She's very beautiful on the outside. But James, she's even more beautiful on the inside, a Godly woman."

Shortly thereafter, and about eight months after our wedding was to have originally occurred, I called her one day in that fall of 1994 and told her of the mistake that I had made. She made it clear that she was not willing to go back to dating. Either I knew what I wanted or I didn't. I assured her that I did. She accepted my second proposal, and we proceeded to set the wedding date—December 1.

There was a period of adjustment though, which we both went through. The patterns of my life had become so ingrained by the reality of being a longtime bachelor that it was a struggle for me at times to learn to think of myself as part of a couple. Dorothy was very patient with me as we grew together spiritually and as husband and wife. But there is one thing that has occurred that is surprising. I can barely make any decisions on my own as it relates to what I wear for business or formal occasions. I *thought* I was a pretty good dresser, but apparently that was in my own mind! I've learned it is better to get her input on the "front end" of a choice—something I would assume most husbands know.

I don't think that I suddenly was any worse at picking my clothes or that she was any more difficult about my selections, I just think I wasn't nearly as aware of—or concerned about—things like that when I was single as I am now. I would always dress nicely, but I didn't have the immediate feedback if something wasn't just right. As a result, after a period of her feedback as to some of my selections, I've become almost paralyzed in trying to select what I should wear.

I will sometimes lay out a suit before I get into the shower, along with my dress shirt, shoes, and tie. Inevitably I will come out, Dorothy will be nowhere in sight, and the tie will be different. I will wear the tie she's chosen, and without fail, at least once that day, someone will say, "Hey—great tie!" So, therefore I've pretty much given up on dressing myself. After all, Dorothy was a fashion merchandising major in college—duh!

Dorothy has been a wonderful soul mate. My only regret about our marriage is that I didn't meet her and marry her earlier. She reminds me of Ruth in the Bible, because she is so obedient and faithful in her daily walk with the Lord, and so loyal and loving with me. Her biggest challenge with me and my lifestyle, she says, is that I allow myself to get too busy. Some of our nicest times have been when we've vacationed, at our favorite place in the Bahamas—Great Exuma—or at a friend's waterfront home near Chincoteague, Virginia. Those times seem to soothe my soul and allow me to disconnect from the busyness of my world, and just enjoy my time alone with her. When we're in town, I'm still trying to learn to do a better job to just stop every now and then and reflect on things—to slow down and enjoy simple moments, time with her and my family, all the daily joys of life. It's a process for me—but I'm getting better.

She likes to tell the story of our ninth anniversary. I returned home late from broadcasting in Los Angeles, and she decided that she wanted to create a romantic mood, and welcome me home with a path of rose petals, beginning at the front door all the way to our bedroom.

She heard the door open, and awaited my arrival, knowing that I would rush up the stairs. Seconds turned into minutes. No James in the doorway. Finally, she came to the top of the stairs, and saw me stooped over, with broom in hand sweeping up the rose petals!

"What are you doing?"

"Hey, Sweetie. I just got in and found that somebody dropped flower petals all over the floor, and I didn't want you to have to worry about cleaning them up." Oh, well...talk about being too busy to smell the roses!

I'm so bad around the house that using a dustpan is one of the only things that I can do. I can't cook, and I'm not very good with my hands as a handyman. When I was young, my parents had asked me to put in a glass shower door, including caulking it—I've blocked out whatever else was involved. I did a terrible job, and from that point forward when something similar came up that needed attention, my family was quick to say, "James isn't very good with his hands," and would send me instead to go wax the floors. Again.

Dorothy also claims that my mother turned me into a very high maintenance individual, and I think she's right. My mom would even fix my plate when I ate at her house. Dorothy grew close to my mother, a development for which I am so grateful. For us, our experience was the exact opposite to many stories that we hear about how one spouse or the other feels about in-laws. Dorothy and Mom spoke by telephone nearly every day, and many days we went to my Mom's house to spend time with her and soak up all the wisdom she had. That occurred every Sunday in my offseason as we went to Mom's house for dinner. Even during her last years, battling health issues, Mom would have a feast for the family to enjoy on Sundays, reminiscent of the scenes from the movie *Soul Food*—where Mom, the matriarch, expected everyone to show up, enjoy good food and fellowship, and hear her thoughts on whatever was going on in our family, and dispense her advice, whether we asked for it or not!

At the same time, she gave us our distance and let us live our lives as husband and wife; yet we both cherished the fact that Mom was always around as a sounding board. She would sometimes mediate as to something Dorothy and I had going on, but *only if asked*. Both of us valued her opinion.

The only problem for me was that despite me being a mama's boy, she never took sides, at least in my favor. If anything, her initial assumption was that Dorothy was right and that I was messing up. If I was wrong she had no compunction about telling me pointedly that I was wrong. She would always open the Bible and start to ask me pointed questions: "Are you honoring your wife?" "Are you showing her respect?"

Now that Mom has passed we have continued to read the Bible and pray together, and to grow together through Bible study sessions we attend every Wednesday at our church which help to strengthen our understanding of how relationships are to work, reinforcing the Scripture, how can two walk together lest they be agreed (see Amos 3:3).

I'm thrilled I'm not a bachelor any longer.

CHAPTER 10

THE RIGHT WAY . . .

Do not think of yourself more highly than you
ought, but rather think of yourself with sober
judgment, in accordance with the measure
of faith God has given you.

Romans 12:3 (NIV)

During the time I was dating Dorothy, following my disappointment with not becoming the lead play-by-play announcer for college basketball or the studio host for March Madness, I still stayed on with CBS. I was even more determined to continue to push ahead, certain that I would end up wherever God wanted me. In the meantime, I reminded myself that God had me where He wanted me now. It was important to me that I embraced that and realized that He knew my future. My responsibility was to do the best I could for two reasons: I owed it to the people and the task at hand; and God would use it to prepare me for wherever He wanted me, and whatever He had next for me to do.

And so, I remained true to what I was doing, and tried my best to remain patient. I was still working NFL games as a play-by-play announcer at CBS, with a broadcast partner by the name of John Robinson, the former head coach of the University of Southern California and the Los Angeles Rams.

One week, we were in Atlanta to do a game for the Falcons, and Coach suggested we go shopping at a store where athletes would go whenever in Atlanta, Friedman's, where they could find the latest shoe fashions in larger sizes. I hadn't fully made a total transition to conservative attire— at times I still liked to dress with the panache I thought I showed at Harvard. So Coach Robinson and I decided to visit Friedman's. After a quick review of what they had to offer, he held up a pair of shoes.

"JB, you have *got* to buy these." I protested. They were, after all, lime green, snakeskin shoes. I pointed out that *he* wasn't buying a pair. "Of course not, those are totally *you*. Not me. Those are perfect for you."

I couldn't recognize at that moment that I was being played. "Coach, I have nothing to wear with lime green, snakeskin dress shoes."

"You will. You can just have a suit made." I still haven't fully grasped why I bought those shoes. They were awful and I knew it, but I allowed myself to be talked into it.

After we were married, Dorothy went through my closet, taking inventory on what she had to work with, and what would need changing and supplementing. She happened upon the lime green shoes—how could she miss them—which I was unfortunate enough to have placed next to a pair of oxblood-colored snakeskin dress shoes that I had added to my collection recently.

"Where do you even wear these shoes?" Dorothy asked.

"I never have. I don't have anything or anywhere to wear them. Maybe, however, if you and I were going—"

Her interruption was polite, quick, and resolute:

"There is nowhere with me that you can ever wear these shoes. It is never appropriate for you to wear these shoes anywhere around me." She went to throw them away.

"Hold on there, Sweetie. I was thinking that I might get an outfit—"

"An *outfit!* Oh, no, you don't. You are not getting anything that could possibly go with these." I could see the battle was lost, but still held out some hope for the war.

"Let me see if I can have them dyed." Sure enough, I took them out and had them dyed black, at least partially salvaging my lime green shoes so that they would see the light of another day. And I ended up wearing them to some black tie events after that.

I think that was the only time that I allowed Coach Rob to lead me astray. I continued to press ahead with CBS, while making time for my personal life. One of the primary areas of my personal life that I always made a priority had been

Katrina, who was spending weekends with me, as well as a number of weekdays.

As she got older, she began asking if she could have friends over to spend the night on occasion. That was fine, and it all went smoothly, without incident, the first couple of times. On one particular weekend, however, she had about four of her girlfriends over to spend the night at my DC townhouse. The next morning, I thought I was being the good dad when I asked them what they would like for breakfast. It wasn't until their mothers picked them up that I learned, from the mothers, that you don't ask seven-year-old girls what they would like for breakfast, you give them one option and make that one meal for everyone.

Katrina, knowing my cooking capabilities, chose Rice Krispies. The others really should have taken her cue, but instead asked for oatmeal, buttermilk pancakes, grits, and Cream of Wheat. I was at the stove scrambling not only to act as if I knew how to make any of them, but also to prepare them simultaneously.

I finished with a triumph as Katrina looked on, impressed. The girls with the oatmeal, grits, and Cream of Wheat all had the same experience. One put her spoon into the bowl and held it—and the bowl—upside down over the table without a drop of the gummy oatmeal coming out, while another stood her spoon upright in the Cream of Wheat, and we timed how long it took for the spoon to fall ever-so-slowly before it touched the side of the bowl. We measured the time in tens of minutes. The little girl with the pancakes quickly figured that she had gotten the one thing that came out right, until she cut into the first pancake and the uncooked batter inside gushed out and across the plate.

Everyone ended up with Rice Krispies.

When she was about eight, I took Katrina with me on a cruise. Bob Costas hosted one week-long cruise each year on Norwegian Cruise Lines, as I recall, and I filled in for him two or three times. On one of those, I took Katrina with me. We were able to enjoy some time to ourselves and also spend time on the cruise with a number of terrific people, including Byron Scott, the late Dennis Johnson, and their wives. After a night or two, we were into a routine and I was feeling pretty good about how things seemed to be going. Dad had everything under control. There would be no more backing myself into a corner over meals, like had happened at the slumber party.

Until we headed down for dinner to meet the others, and we both realized that I had no idea how to help fix a little girl's hair for going out in public.

Not sure what else to do, I called a friend's cabin. I asked if his wife would mind doing Katrina's hair. She was gracious enough to accept—a good thing since Katrina was upset at the possibility of going to dinner with the mess that I had made of her hair. She attempted to do her hair, but ultimately we headed down to dinner with Katrina still feeling uncomfortable but trying to make the best of it. No sooner were we seated than Byron Scott's wife, Anita, told Katrina to come with her. I could hear her laughing and muttering as they walked away, "I don't know why men can't do little girls' hair, but..."

Katrina came back with her hair all neatly in place, and much happier for the rest of dinner.

In 1994, the unthinkable happened. CBS, a broadcast partner of the NFL since 1956, lost the rights to the NFC package to the then-fledgling FOX network. The NFC, the commonly used acronym for the National Football Conference—consisting of half of the NFL's thirty-two teams, was the crown jewel of the NFL's television properties. With teams like the New York Giants, the Dallas Cowboys, the San Francisco 49ers, the Chicago Bears and the then–Los Angeles Rams, the NFC contains many of the marquee, old line teams of the NFL, with established fan bases and mega-markets. With this turn of events, however, those of us at CBS who had been working NFL games were potentially out in the cold, as NBC retained the rights to the AFC (the American Football Conference) which constitutes the other half of the League.

In an instant, CBS had no NFL broadcast property at all.

Sure enough, CBS decided to retain Jim Nantz and Greg Gumbel, and a handful of other broadcasters to handle the other sports remaining in their portfolio. The rest of us were scrambling. I was standing on God's promises, which at that moment seemed to be the only assurance I had. I began wondering if I should head back to local television, or maybe I could work as one of FOX's play-by-play broadcasters. They had already signed a number of big names in broadcasting, but maybe I could fill some sort of role.

Little did I realize, however, that what seemed to be a bleak hour would turn into the biggest professional opportunity with which I had ever been presented. FOX had put together three-quarters of its Sunday pre-game show, with Terry Bradshaw, Howie Long, and Jimmy Johnson. Those were such strong personalities, however, that there were concerns about finding the right host for the show. Ed Goren, who had worked at CBS, was brought over as one of the top executives, and he began lobbying for me to join the show. Finally, they extended an offer—at a bargain salary, but I was thrilled for the opportunity. Amazing. To go from the disappointment of not being promoted within CBS's basketball show to CBS losing the NFL, to joining FOX as the studio host with Terry, Howie, and Jimmy—I was pinching myself.

It was an opportunity that I believed I needed to follow through with, one of the most important self-checks I had to conduct whether I was mature enough in my Christian walk to handle all of the glitz and glamour of Los Angeles. DC is admittedly a big city, but for me it is small because I'm usually at home with my family. Would the bright lights of Hollywood lead me off the path I wanted to continue to walk? I decided not to move out there—I would fly out on Friday afternoons, get acclimated to Pacific time on Saturday, and then fly back to DC on Monday. By the second year I was with FOX, I was married to Dorothy, which helped to keep me grounded.

Each Sunday before I went on the air for the FOX NFL Sunday broadcast, I would call my mom and Dorothy and they would lead me in prayer. I understand just how important it is to have on the full armor of God to do all I could to make my colleagues look good. I was taught that at an early age by my mom, who also taught me Proverbs 22:6, and has been living it out ever since: "Train up a child in the way he should go: and when he is old, he will not depart from it" (KJV). Since Sundays were a full workday for me, and I was missing my normal weekly time to worship God in church, I decided to make Wednesdays during the season into my Sundays, and regularly attended church back home on that day.

Things couldn't have gone better on the set. Terry, Howie, Jimmy, and I got along great both off the air and on, and we were number one from the time that we went on the air. That first day, all pumped and nervously excited to be a part of a new show that many football fans were waiting to see, and critique, we were a little uptight as the nine o'clock hour approached in Los Angeles—twelve o'clock on the east coast—and we would go live to our viewing audience. The director began his countdown. "One minute." Everyone was quiet, and then good old Terry Bradshaw, as only he could, began giving tips. He turned to Jimmy.

"Jimmy, this isn't like coaching. You don't want your lips to get dry. That's the most important thing you can do before you go on. Have soft, supple lips." We started to laugh, but Howie nodded. Terry pulled a round tin of Carmex lip balm out of his pocket and offered it to Jimmy. Jimmy applied it and passed it back.

"Thirty seconds." Terry began using it himself, as then Howie did the same with some that he had. Terry didn't offer me any lip balm as he'd done with my colleagues. I hit him on the shoulder and said, "Hey, you didn't offer me any." He pulled out the lip balm, looked at it, looked at my lips once, then said, "Hold out both hands, you'll need a lot of his for those lips."

"Fifteen seconds."

The cameras came up in September 1994, to find the inaugural show of FOX NFL Sunday broken up with laughter. That was the atmosphere of our show each and every Sunday. Much like a locker room atmosphere, no one was exempt from getting teased.

That first year was an action-packed one, including plenty of growing pains for FOX and us. One of the most memorable for Howie was the time that I had to read the teleprompter—while it ran backward.

That opening moment as we went on the air as well as that whole first year, looking back, was a microcosm of our experience on FOX. We had fun, letting our genuine friendships spill over onto the airwaves. Our goal at FOX was to be light-hearted, to educate the viewers without them realizing it, to "sugar-coat the education pill" that we tried to give the viewers each week. David Hill, the chairman and CEO of FOX sports, was as creative, smart, and talent sensitive an executive as I've seen in the broadcast business.

For as close as we were, however, they would never accept an invitation of mine to come over and spend the night at my home, even though I promised not to make pancakes—or oatmeal. None of us lived in Los Angeles, so we all commuted every weekend. When we would go to dinner,

I would always wear a coat and tie, even in that Southern California heat. I had finally learned my lesson about dress. They would look nice, but invariably wear jeans. Jimmy, of course, would always look like something right out of the Florida Keys, wearing a Tommy Bahama shirt.

They even had the production guys put together a spoof at my expense: they were all out at the marina in casual shirts and swim trunks during a vignette that we were filming, and I came out in a suit and tie, then sat in the lotus position, looking focused and serious, while they had a pool party all around me. Terry came to stay with Howie in Virginia once, and we've all visited Jimmy's spread down in the Keys. But when I offered for them to come stay with us—they all were busy. Every night for twelve years. They would always protest that they would be happy to come, except that they were afraid that their evening attire would be laid out on the bed—dinner jackets and ascots. They said that I'm just a certifiable square.

Howie says that on television you can't hide who you are—it inevitably comes out. My goal has always been to be the guy that America wanted to invite into their living room. Even if it meant that I'm something of a square.

Another of those vignettes that FOX had us tape was on a boat. There we all were, dressed casually—even me. The boat stopped and we were going to fish at that spot. I turned to the others and delivered my line, so stiff that even I realized how badly it had gone: "Gee . . . Guys . . . how did you come up on this spot?" They have never let me live it down.

After a couple of years, I did have the chance to go Hollywood for FOX. I hosted *The World's Funniest!* for two years

ROLE OF A LIFETIME

in the late 1990s, and it was remarkable how many folks recognize me more for doing that show than co-hosting the #1 NFL pregame show! Especially children and mothers. I was excited that David Hill gave me the opportunity to host that show for the Entertainment Division and it seems to have been nothing but positive from the viewers and my colleagues—well, except for Tony Kornheiser, a good friend of mine.

I was driving around town one day and heard Tony start out on a rant on his radio show.

"What is JB doing, anyway! He doesn't need the money, yet here he is hosting 'When Animals Attack' or something! I thought he was a smart guy, but then I saw him the other night on 'When Animals Beat Up on Each Other' and now I'm losing respect for him by the minute!" I could hardly drive I was laughing so hard, and thankfully most viewers did not seem to share Tony's opinion. It was a fun experience that allowed me a different venue than sports. I strive to help them see me the way I try to be—warm, sincere, truly caring about those around me—special people every one of them. If I can get any of that across, I have succeeded.

I also had the chance to act in everything from a made-for-television movie with Bob Newhart and Kelsey Grammer, and to "act" in a couple of animated shows, FOX's *The Simpsons* and *King of the Hill*.

In the episode of *The Simpsons*, I ran into Bart Simpson in an NFL locker room, and the writers perfectly captured the response I receive so often in the public.

"I'm Bart Simpson. Who are you?"

"I'm James Brown."

"Oh, the Godfather of Soul! All right! [sings] I feeel gooood."

"No, not that James Brown."

"Oh, the one that was the Hall of Fame running back for the Cleveland Browns? That Jim Brown?"

"No, not that one, either."

"Oh, you're the no-talent talking head on Sunday afternoon!"

Sometimes James Brown can be a tough name to go through life with.

My nephew, Ahmaud Dairsow, was in our home several months later and saw a picture that I have hanging on my wall that is one of the animated frames from *King of the Hill.* In the episode, the writers were accommodating enough of me—since I don't drink—to substitute their usual beers for Cokes, which our characters drank while they stood around. Ahmaud wasn't to be fooled, however, when he looked at the picture.

"Hey, look," he said to Dorothy, "it's 'Keg of the Hill!'" He paused. "But who's the black guy?"

Howie, Terry, and Jimmy all were getting the chance to do advertising, and I was hoping to do some as well. A beer company invited me to do a commercial with Terry early in my tenure at FOX, and I was ecstatic. They had come out with an inflatable line of "easy chairs," with cup holders in the armrests with the logo and colors of the various NFL teams. I told them that I'd rather not have a beer in the cup holder, and they graciously agreed.

The commercial began airing and, I must admit, I was pretty proud. James Brown, in a commercial, with Terry Bradshaw.

Until my niece called. And even though she was only ten at the time, she could always be very direct.

"Uncle James, how could you do that!?" I was lost.

"Do what?"

"Do what you *did*." She was so agitated she couldn't get it all out at once.

"What, sweetie? What did I do?" I was still confused, but getting worried.

"The commercial." The light started to come on for me.

"Oh honey, that was for Super Bowl team products, for inflatable chairs."

"Uncle James, it was about beer!"

I smiled despite myself, at her misunderstanding. "Honey, I didn't have a beer can in my hand. I wasn't promoting the use of beer. I told them I wouldn't do anything with alcohol. This was just for the inflatable chairs."

"Uncle James, please. I can't believe that you're trying to convince me of that. Where do you have to go to get the coupons for the chairs? At convenience stores in the beer section, right? In front of the beer company display, right? Or at a liquor store, right?" I wasn't smiling at her naïveté anymore, but rather, was cringing at mine, and that it was taking my ten-year-old niece to tell me so. She didn't let up, though. "Do you remember coming to speak to my school last fall? What was that for?"

"The D.A.R.E. Program," I whispered. I had gone to her school on a hot, September day and given a presentation to her classmates. She was so proud that I was there and was a big help in dabbing my perspiring brow during the presentation as I spoke.

"That's right. Dare to stay off alcohol and drugs, and then...how could you, Uncle James!"

From that point forward I vowed that I would not do any commercials that had to do with anything that could be a potential stumbling block or source of addiction for someone else. And I haven't, despite having had some opportunities to do so since. Thanks to the clear thinking of a very dear and very wise ten-year-old.

I loved FOX, and I loved the guys. It was perfect, and we were having a blast. We joked around together—Howie, Terry, and Jimmy loved to tease me about my diet. I have a very large frame, and well—it's a large frame. Howie likes to tell me that they "had to kill a whole family of gabardine just to clothe" me, or that watching me diet is amusing, because I "have the willpower of a common housefly—it'll land on anything!"

We had our serious moments, too, however. Terry and I even had some meaningful talks when he wanted to talk to me as he went through the pain of a divorce. One of the highest compliments he paid me as a friend was asking me to sit in the car in front of his LA apartment and be a listener as he poured out his heart, and then asked to close the evening with a prayer. I was thankful I had something relevant to say and pray because of my efforts in studying the Bible in weekly classes at my church. We were having special times on the set, and I was growing off the set as well.

My goal through all of that was simply to be who I was created to be. Some people are designed to be the stars, while others are designed to support them. All are important. The reality, I believed, was that our show would be a success if the viewers enjoyed Terry, Howie, and Jimmy. It's all about what we bring to the table that makes another look good.

I learned that truth years before from Coach Wooten, who would stop and rewind the film so that we could watch—for the third and fourth time—the player who had left his feet to knock the ball out of bounds to help our team, or set the pick that led to the pass that led to a basket. It wouldn't ever make the box score, and most people would never notice it, but Coach always did. And he made sure that we did. He made sure it would stay with us when he wasn't.

That's true in life as well. Even if we're not the star and no one really sees what we do, there are others who see our contributions. Those in the know will see what we do. And even when we don't think they do, God sees—He is always in the know. I take solace in that, plus it also causes me to go out of my way to make sure that I openly appreciate those whose contributions might not be noticed by others. The bellhop or the housekeeper at my many hotel stays, or the cab driver, or the grips or statisticians on the broadcast sets.

I know them all by name in my regular spots—at my hotel, on the set, or on my route. I make it a point to do that. They deserve my time and respect no less than anyone else. They have remarkable and interesting life stories. They, too, need to know that they are someone special. I try to make sure they know that they are—to me.

It's an important part of the role I know God wants me to play.

CHAPTER 11

...AT THE RIGHT TIME

Likewise, teach the older women to be reverent in
the way they live, not to be slanderers or addicted to
much wine, but to teach what is good. Then they can
train the younger women to love their husbands and
children, to be self-controlled and pure, to be busy
at home, to be kind, and to be subject to their husbands, so that no one will malign the word of God.

Titus 2:3–5 (NIV)

Tuesday, September 11, 2001 was a traumatic day for
our nation.

It was a long day, while as a nation we watched and heard
reports coming in from everywhere early that morning that
a plane had crashed into one of the towers of the World
Trade Center. And then minutes later we were horrified with

the report that a second plane had hit the second tower of the World Trade Center. The reports kept coming in and we learned that what we had feared the most—was true. America had been attacked. Television accounts recounted over and over the grim reality of that truth. We prayed unintelligibly through the numbness which had now overcome us.

Much has been said, shared, and written about that day, but memories of that day have flooded me then and in times since—in addition to the obvious shock that I felt, with periods of reflection characterized by a range of emotions—all centering on the safety of my family and how soon could I get home to them. My initial reaction was probably a lot like yours—it felt completely surreal to have my morning filled watching planes flying into buildings; it was hard to believe what we were watching. Then those feelings gave way to fear. Where were the other planes around the country? Were the attacks over? Would they ever be over? The reports kept coming in. Hijacked commercial airliners were used. Other attacks had been orchestrated—one on the Pentagon and another, apparently diverted by passengers on the plane from its intended target, instead crashing in a field near Shanksville, Pennsylvania. Air Force One was en route to DC.

Emotions across the nation and world swirled in confusion and grief. I gathered the faces in my heart of all whom I loved.

I was in San Antonio visiting my brother John at the time. I was very concerned about my family's safety because of the reports of a plane that crashed into the Pentagon. I needed to hear the voices of Dorothy, Katrina, Mom, and the rest of my family. At that moment I needed to reconnect with them that day—it was something more than reassurance that they were okay—it was a search for the reassurance that everything would be okay.

I sighed a huge sigh of relief after the initial calls home to find out that my family was all right, and all I wanted to do was to get home. Nothing else. I wanted to go home. I needed to be home. There were, of course, no flights to be had, as the airlines weren't operating with the aviation system shut down across the nation for security reasons. Cars weren't available to rent in San Antonio, as others had beaten me to the punch.

The executives at FOX called, and they still hadn't gotten an official word from the NFL on whether games would be played that weekend, but if they went ahead with the schedule and the games were played, FOX would need me back in Los Angeles for the studio show. In anticipation of the games being played, FOX advised that they were going to send the car and driver that they used to transport me in LA to come and get me in San Antonio, to assure that I would be back in Los Angeles by the weekend.

I wanted to go home. I needed to be home.

By the time the car arrived at my brother's home in San Antonio, Paul Tagliabue, the Commissioner of the NFL, had just announced that the games for that weekend had been postponed. FOX wouldn't need me in Los Angeles after all, and they offered to have the two drivers, Vincent Sims and Mike Neeley—it turned out that they sent two drivers because of the distance—drive me back to DC. And so the three of us left to make the trip from San Antonio, Texas, to Maryland—Vincent, Mike, and myself.

It was an unforgettable time for me. Every moment since the morning of that Tuesday has been seared in my consciousness. On our way back, we stopped at T.D. Jakes's church in Dallas and worshipped there, sparking a discussion among the three of us about the spiritual ramifications of September 11. As we motored through Arkansas, the events of that day led to an even longer three-way conversation on faith more generally, as well as what it meant to be an American and a citizen of the world in 2001.

That discussion took us through Tennessee and Virginia.

Finally, we arrived in DC. Home, at long last. Mike and Vincent stayed at our home and attended church with my family. We rested a day or so before preparing for the long cross-country trip back to California.

Things were already beginning to change.

Initially we had thought that, after some time at home, I would ride back with them, but FOX had arranged for the rental of a large bus—similar to the type that John Madden uses for his travel—for us to make the trip to Los Angeles: David Blatt, a FOX producer, Dorothy, and me. We took three and a half days to get back across the country, stopping in big cities and small hamlets, doing pieces on the reaction of the people we met along our journey to the terrorist attacks of the prior week.

Edifying and reassuring.

Those were the words that sprang to mind as we journeyed across the nation during those few days, where American flags flew, it seemed, from nearly every building and home. We talked with the typical man- and woman-on-the-street, soliciting and gauging their reactions and current states of mind to the attacks of that day a week ago. The reactions were the same across party lines, educational backgrounds, socio-economic status, ethnicities, and professions: We are all Americans. We don't know what the future holds, but we will get through this—together.

That was the overriding theme of the week, and I was glad to find myself in this unique position to interact with so many around the country so soon after such a tragic event on our soil. It seemed as though those events served to shake, awaken, and unify the collective pride for our land, its people, and the principles upon which our country was founded. The collective soul of our country emerged in one voice. What was right and what was wrong, in the minds of those we met, was very clear. The right way to go as a people—together as a country—was clear to everyone we met along the way.

A fond memory of good people—my fellow Americans.

And in the days which followed in our country, we came together. People from every walk of life—men, women, white- and blue-collar workers, mechanics, company CEO's, teachers, students, people of every race, color, culture, and background, united in one common theme—America. In one unified voice, every member of Congress joined hands on the steps of the U.S. Capitol to sing their allegiance to our country and each other.

The focus of those we spoke to was not on our differences, but on the things that unite us. In the strain of those times, what was right and good about us—things that tied us together as a people—came to the forefront of our thoughts and lives. The healing would take time, but the determination had set in, as only it can in America. The right way was clear. The right way was ahead of us to follow together as a nation, as heroes from every corner of this land rose up where they were needed and began to reach out to each other, to restore our national confidence in ways we had done so many times before, and to rebuild our lives and nation.

My mother described herself as "The Titus Woman." She felt that way because in the little three-chapter book of Titus in the Bible it says, among other things, that the older women teach the young women to love their husbands, to love their children, to teach them how to be good wives and mothers.

Mom formally and informally taught women about marriage, family and sacrifice. She always stressed the importance of making the home a place full of love and caring. Women naturally took to my mother and she was, in turn, naturally attracted to the needs of other women.

She always had the gift of encouragement. She always made others feel better in whatever they were going through in their life at the time. Even as people came by to visit Mom with the intention of lifting her spirits, inevitably they would leave feeling better about themselves because Mom moved their spirits! It was a gift from God—and she allowed it and Him to flow through her—no matter how she felt, to bless others.

The bottom line is, Mom's example was a wonderful model for me. A model of how to treat people, how to encourage them, how to pass along the benefits of experiences I've had. People would call her every day seeking guidance or prayer. If I was ever calling her—or anyone else was calling for that matter—and she was praying, she wouldn't click over to take our call. Those times that she could spend in prayer were sacred times to her. She loved being an encourager—for anyone and everyone. I remember vividly the times when she was praying with conviction for the needs of people that she may not have particularly liked!

Beyond that, she was always receptive to the opportunities where she might be able to help someone in whatever fashion she could—she was very prudent with the gifts and resources that God had given her. She would find homeopathic remedies to help Mr. Washington in her neighborhood, who suffered from a debilitating cancer late in his life. She would never allow him or Mrs. Washington to reimburse her, but would always point out that she was simply "sowing." She would sow her time and her prayers and her money, with purpose. God's purpose. She knew that when she sowed, others would be blessed. When someone would try to repay her, she would say, "Don't make me miss out on my blessing." They never did.

———∞———

I don't know if you would classify them as blessings or not. But I love cars. Classic cars, muscle cars, and hot rods.

I have always loved hot rods, and currently have several—fewer than I owned a couple of years ago, though. But even more than the cars, however, I love the kind of cars enthusiasts call "drivers," as opposed to just "show cars." Going to a car show is my chance to escape from the busyness of my schedule. At car shows everyone is just the guy or gal next door. Nobody cares about titles or positions, or companies for which you work, and nobody puts on any airs of his or her own. If I weren't such an inquisitive soul, always eager to learn as much as I can about people, you'd never know from what walk of life people at these shows came.

I think the thing I like most about cars and being around people who like them also, however, has become the opportunities it provides me to interact with people from a varied spectrum of life experiences, occupations, faiths, and interests. I suppose it's the grease on our hands from working on an engine, changing the oil or a tire—that has a leveling effect—as well as the common interest we all share that brings a diverse group of people together. In any event, I was always taught by my parents to look beyond and behind titles and trappings, and to look toward the person's heart.

Being around car people gives me a chance to do that. At shows we enjoy each other's company: doctors and mechanics, professors and factory workers, it just doesn't matter. That's just how I like it. No pretense or pride, just people.

The spring and summer weekends offer opportunities to go to the local cruise spots—to relive one's teenage years, enjoy the fellowship, and appreciate the many fine restored cars of yesteryear. If you've never experienced going to a cruise night, where car lovers gather to proudly showcase their classic vehicles, then you may think it strange that we find the fragrance of high octane fuel rather soothing. So, after a frenetic week of activities, it's not unusual for me to say to Dorothy, "Hey sweetheart, I'm going to 'smell some gas,'" which is car vernacular for going to enjoy an evening at a local cruise spot!

General Motors created a limited edition Corvette last year, the ZR1. I heard that they may have made as few as twelve hundred of them, with many of those shipped overseas. Because I was one of the spokesmen for GMC, they allowed me to buy one of these limited number rocket ships! Because I had considerably pared down my automobile inventory—I have a 1969 black Camaro named "Black Cherry," an orange 1941 Willys named "Zesst," a black Camaro named "Black Pearl," and now even Dorothy has a black and silver '41 Chevy Cabriolet named "Amazing Love"—I convinced myself that I was able to justify adding this new Corvette to the mix.

One of the top executives at GM was personally approving the VIP list of those who would be offered the opportunity to acquire one of these beauties, and the first car to come off the production line went to Jay Leno. Incidentally, the second one went to the owner of a huge, high-end car auction, who was going to auction it off and give the proceeds to charity. I later heard that the car that he auctioned off received a bid of one million dollars. (The next time you hear the cliché about beauty salon gossip, remember it's not gender based—come listen to the tales that car guys hanging out at a car show will spin.)

Making things more palatable and easier to justify, I wasn't scheduled to receive my car until the following January, allowing me several months to demonstrate my new and more responsible approach to the stewardship of resources around the house. And then I received the call. Because of my spokesperson role, I was receiving car number seventeen off the line and that it would be ready in the next couple of weeks. I needed to remold my image quicker than anticipated, in the eyes of two of the ladies in my life whom I couldn't fool.

It arrived, and it was beautiful. I had the guys down at Bubbas East Coast Hot Rods & Customs take one of my other cars, and surreptitiously placed the ZR1, under a cover, in its place in the garage. Dorothy knew that it was coming—someday—but I wanted a chance to tell her how shocked I was that it arrived.

I had initially heard that Jay Leno was going to get car number two off the assembly line. But when my brother John told me that he heard Jay on *The Tonight Show* talking about his excitement in waiting for his new ZR1 to arrive, I decided to give him a call to rub it in a bit. Since I already had mine in hand, I wanted to express my sincerest regret that his had not arrived yet.

Jay Leno is one of the great people of show business, or anywhere, frankly. He is just true salt of the earth. Just a regular nice guy. Who also happens to have a lot of really nice cars that I had a chance to see at his garage in Burbank, California—an unbelievable collection.

I first met Jay when I was in Los Angeles on a regular basis. I happened to go to a muscle car and hot rod show held in a park out there and all of a sudden, a guy pulled up in a car that looked like a bullet. No entourage, no posse. Just Jay Leno out for a drive.

Some time after that he invited me out to see his cars, which he keeps in an airplane hangar. I was going to be on *The Tonight Show* that night, so we were passing time until we needed to meet with the writers. I was marveling at his collection when he announced that he had to fill one up. "Come on, let's go for a ride," he said. We climbed into his Stanley Steamer—1906, as I recall—and headed down to the gas station, at a speed far faster than I thought that car could, or should, be traveling. Just a couple of guys headed down the road wearing their old-fashioned automobile goggles. It was quite a picture.

Later that evening, Terry, Howie, and I went on the show. Jay had been hanging out with us in our dressing rooms, where I was eating the watermelon that they had brought me—I was on a special diet and had requested it. Terry and Howie had a variety of other fruit set out for them, but no watermelon. Jay said that he was sure that there was a joke there but that he wasn't going to touch it. Once we were in front of the audience, Jay greeted us, and I thanked him for his hospitality, but I was wondering why—out of the three of us—I was the only one who had been given watermelon.

Jay just about jumped up from behind his desk, saying, "You ordered that watermelon, not me!" Terry and Howie just sat back and howled. He is such a good guy, but it was fun to turn the table on him for a moment and try to get him to squirm.

When I called Jay's office I merely wanted his voicemail, to let Jay know Christmas had come early for me with the ZR1 delivery. Just one car guy sharing his excitement with another car guy. Plus, I wanted his voicemail because, although I had been a guest on *The Tonight Show* years ago, I wasn't completely sure that he would remember me.

I spoke to his assistant and asked that she pass a message along to Jay. "This is James Brown. Would you tell him, please, that I got my new ZR1 and really love it." She asked the color and I told her—cyber gray. She asked me to hang on. I assumed she was putting me through to voicemail.

"JB, how are you?!" Jay's voice boomed through the line.

"I'm doing great. Hey, I was just calling like a little kid excited with his new toy, to let you know that my ZR1 arrived, and I just know that you are going to love yours—when it arrives."

"I got mine—it's cyber gray, too. Isn't it great the way it drives, JB?"

"Well, I haven't actually driven mine yet. I was calling to tell you that I was number seventeen—how do you already have yours?"

"I got number *one!*" So much for relying on the gossip around the garage.

———— ◦◦◦ ————

Things were still going very smoothly at FOX, and I really enjoyed the people who were there. I also enjoyed spending time with many of the people in the NFL who I had the opportunity to get to know on a more personal level. For instance, I have always admired New England Patriots team owner Bob Kraft. His team-oriented approach in his highly successful businesses and, of course, his football team has led to a modern-day dynasty. His head coach, Bill Belichick, has a way of getting everyone to buy into his system and play a specific role, much the way I have tried to approach my position as the studio host, as well as other roles I have played throughout my life. The Coach Wootten way. Bill Belichick has taken a number of players who've been starters on other teams and inspired them to be valuable role players with the Patriots way of football. A tribute to teamwork.

Brett Favre is another that I have admired for years for a number of reasons. Brett is an intense competitor who was remarkably durable in a brutally physical sport. He confronted his demons of addiction with candor, openness, and directness and worked his way through them. I love watching the kidlike enthusiasm with which he played the game, but even more than that, I like watching him, knowing what he has overcome and left behind in his wake.

Of course, then there is Tony Dungy. I think one of the reasons that I was immediately drawn to Tony Dungy was because he reminded me so much of Coach Wootten. Coach Wootten believed that he was a teacher and it was counterproductive in that role for him to belittle players. Of course, the first time that I heard Tony say that his parents were teachers, and by their example he viewed his primary function as a coach to be that of a teacher, I saw the similarity. Coach Wootten used to say, "Whoever makes basketball work will make life work."

When Tony went on then to say that he believed that players want to be successful and that he was just trying to give them the tools to get there, that clinched it for me. And I can honestly say that I have never heard—or heard of— Tony cursing to get his players to perform to a higher level, a championship level. Just like Coach Wootten. It seems to me that we have come to expect that the best and the most effective way to "motivate" players is for coaches to engage in profanity-laced tirades. Oh, I know it is the style of many coaches, but I've been most impressed by the likes of Tony Dungy, UCLA great John Wooden, and my high school coach Morgan Wootten, among others, who showed that they can be excellent teachers, getting championship results without filthy language.

While I was staying busy with life at FOX and in and around the NFL, I received a call at home in February 2005. Mom had been taken to the hospital in a "code blue" status, and the doctors were very guarded about her condition. Dorothy, on her way to the hospital, began praying and pleading fervently with God, "It's not her time." God obviously agreed, because we were able to keep my mom for a while longer—and she ultimately went back home. In the meantime, we wanted to somehow tell her as a family, after that close call, just how much she meant to us. And so we decided to throw her a seventieth birthday party—the one at which I found myself emotionally choked up and unable to speak for several seconds—the theme of which was drawn from Proverbs 31:28a, "Her children arise up, and call her blessed" (KJV).

The birthday celebration was wonderful. Both the family and friends had a chance to tell Mom how special she was in each of their lives and to take a moment to pray over her, and they allowed me the chance, and privilege, to speak last to conclude the event.

"As everyone before me has noted, the common thread through all of what you had to say is that my mother is not a phony or one who puts on airs. With her, black is black and white is white and there is no gray. There is right and wrong. There is a right way and a wrong way. The road she has traveled has been marked by examples of the right way.

"I guess the best thing you could say about me, and the natural thing, is that I'm a 'Mama's Boy.' As far as I'm concerned, that is the highest compliment with which you could bestow me, because I do love her." It was the highest compliment because of the incredible example she's been, sacrificing for her family in every way possible. Placing her children above her personal desires.

Mom closed things with her comments. "I am grateful for all of you, for your being here and spending time with me. I love each one of you. And I thank God for the precious gift that each of you are, and I pray for all of you every day. But while I am glad to hear all of these things, I want you to remember that this is a celebration and not a funeral, so enjoy yourselves today. Also, I must say that to God be the glory, not me. For the Bible says to give honor where honor is due, and He deserves that honor."

In part because of the urging of Mom and others around me, I am trying to get better with the allocation of my time. I really am. Dorothy will tell you that I still stay too busy, but I think she would acknowledge that I have been getting better over time to try and carve out moments just to spend with her. One of those occasions came a couple of years ago when we went to a black tie affair at Congressional Country Club in Maryland. It was a wonderful occasion, not the least of which was because Dorothy and I were together unrelated to any business obligations of mine. Dorothy made it clear that evening that she enjoyed being with me and doing more things as a couple—and she was right.

As the evening was winding down, we said our good-byes and went outside to get our car. I still remember as we walked outside standing under the porte cochere, waiting for our car to be pulled around, thinking how nice it all had been. I hardly noticed the rain, or that I had stepped out from under the protective cover into it. It was just one of those perfect evenings, I reflected.

My thoughts were interrupted by a commotion behind me. Other guests, who were also waiting for their cars to be brought around, had begun to laugh. I looked around. And then down. I was standing in a puddle of water that had gathered from the rain. There was black water pooling around my shoes—which were now turning lime green. The rain was washing the dye off my snakeskin shoes, leaving me standing there in a black tux, with lime green shoes. Those shoes didn't make it through the door again before Dorothy had them in the trash. I didn't have the heart to admit to Coach Rob when I saw him again that he'd gotten me yet again, years later, with the same pair of shoes.

One of the questions most frequently asked of me is, "why did you leave FOX?" As I've stated earlier, I was not looking to leave. The FOX experience was excellent in every way—a wonderful twelve-year marriage with the number one pregame show. I expected to end my broadcasting career at FOX.

However, I was not aware that I was about to enter a "new season" in my career.

When CBS entered the picture and put an amazing offer

on the table, it created a very tough decision, one that I anguished over. The only way to resolve this was for me to talk with my family, pray about the matter and to be patient in waiting for the answer.

In the end, when my decision was made, I had a real peace in my heart and clarity in my mind, knowing that CBS was the answer.

While leaving so many friends and colleagues at FOX was emotional, I was excited about working for Sean McManus, (President, CBS News and President, CBS Sports) and Tony Petitti, (Executive Vice President, CBS Sports and Executive Producer, CBS Sports), reuniting with colleagues I had started with in the business, and embracing the challenge of helping *The NFL Today* pregame show become the best it could be.

It was the right way to go.

CHAPTER 12

GOD ALWAYS WINS

Heaven sent me a wonderful,
very special, beautiful gift
Heaven sent me a very wonderful,
supernatural, special friend.
Donnie McClurkin, "Special Gift"

Although I was disappointed to be leaving FOX, I was glad to be back with CBS—especially given that Mom's health issues worsened during the time I made the decision to switch. It also meant I would be closer on weekends when and if I was needed. This was such a time.

It was December, 2005, when she had to be taken to the hospital, as she was struggling with various health complications that the doctors couldn't monitor or control while she was at home. It was hard to see her that way in the hospital. She had always been so strong, such an encourager and example. But I was reminded, as I looked at her, of the times I had heard her encourage others so frequently with her knowledge of Scripture, especially the passage that tells us that death is not the end, but the beginning: to be absent from the body is to be present with the Lord (See 2 Cor. 5:8).

And yet still, I couldn't think of letting go. A *mama's boy* through and through.

She was in the hospital for six months and, in that process, showed me as much about how to live in how she handled her dying as I have seen even in many successful examples of people living today. Despite all of the pain and challenges of the ravages of diabetes, despite the three-inch needles searching for marrow, despite pulmonary hypertension and kidney dialysis, she never once complained. Never once.

My siblings and I spent the nights with her, we watched over her, we gave care beyond the nursing staff, and yet through it all, she never complained. In fact, she took to heart the teaching of Paul in 1 Thessalonians 5:16–18, "Rejoice evermore. Pray without ceasing. In every thing give thanks: for this is the will of God in Christ Jesus concerning you" (KJV).

On the evening of December 28 I received a phone call from the hospital. Caroline, the night nurse on duty, told me that my mom was lucid and her vital signs were good but my mom had asked her to call and tell us that Jesus had visited her. Jesus did not want her struggling any longer and he was ready for her. They had prayed together and mom gave her instructions on final plans and preparations for her funeral.

When we arrived at the hospital in the very early hours of the morning it was clear to all of us that a wonderful visitation had indeed occurred. My mom's room was filled with an aura and fragrance of holy presence. She was calm and serene and, although she had never before discussed her funeral wishes in detail, she was completely in-charge, organized and clear about how everything was to be taken care of.

Right up until the day that she died, her faith in Christ remained her clear focus. Her common mantra when people would mention me and my worldly success to her was, "The thing I'm most proud of James for is that he knows Jesus Christ as his Lord and Savior." The room was filled with Scriptures—Alicia had printed them from her computer, eight and a half by eleven inch testimonies to Mom's faith surrounded the otherwise spartan room. Mom was living out the truth of those verses to the very end. Truths such as that in Psalms 118:17, which states, "I shall not die, but live, and declare the works of the LORD" (KJV), an acknowledgement to her zest for life in all circumstances.

She was a ray of sunshine on her hospital floor, growing close to her nurses and all those on staff who came into contact with her. She drew their attention because of her gift of encouragement, and the uncommon strength and determi-

nation she displayed through her painful ordeal. Bill Cosby
and I had become closer friends when I was doing a syndicated issues-oriented TV show that discussed topics of the
day through the lens of African-Americans. Bill, of course,
has thought deeply and spoken widely about this topic, and
we developed a friendship through that. When he heard my
mom was in the hospital, he wanted to visit.

The favor that God showed her through her afflictions drew
many people to her, including Cosby. When he found out
that Mom was in the hospital, he mentioned that he was
going to be in DC performing at the Kennedy Center, and
asked if he could go to visit her. It was a Sunday morning
that he planned to visit with her. I offered to pick him up on
my way to church, but I got a call from my mom saying he
was already in her room, having caught a taxi cab to the hospital. While I had cautioned him that she was having breath-
ing difficulties, when my sister and family got to her room,
we heard her laughing heartily at the yarns only Bill Cosby
could spin—that sight brought smiles to our faces. While Bill
Cosby brought joy into her life that day, Mom shared wisdom and understanding with him.

But once those nurses and staff members got to Mom's
room, they probably didn't find what they were expecting—
someone who needed to be encouraged and cared for—as she
was always the one trying to lift others up and help them in
their lives. She would pray for them, give them counsel, and
look for any other way that she could edify them. Just what
Paul told Titus and the other believers to do.

Finally, in March of 2006, Mom was released from the hospital and she was able to be at the home she loved. But she developed an infection and it was only a matter of days until Mom was back in the hospital.

She was treated for the infection and after two week was released again. Not forty-five minutes after Mom arrived home, I received a call from Alicia. "You need to come—Mom's in pulmonary arrest. They are working on her at her house."

When I got to the house, the paramedics were feverishly working on Mom, trying to revive her. As I sat in the living room praying for her, a young man approached me and asked me if I wanted him to continue his efforts at reviving her as they took her to the hospital. As I looked up, I hadn't recognized the young man as my neighbor, Michael Cardozo. He was a teenager working as an EMT, and he knew of my mom's love through our family. I said yes, and he proceeded to work on her as they took her out of the house and put her on the gurney that was positioned next to her beloved bed of tulips, in their vibrant yellows and pinks.

She spent six weeks after that in a coma. Mom lived six weeks after this incident, which was five weeks, five days longer than any of the doctors or nurses thought she would.

We all took the opportunity in early June to whisper into her ear. "Mom, we're going to be okay. If you've made the decision that you want to go home and be with the Lord, we understand, we love you. We'll see you in heaven."

Sure enough, the Lord took her to her true home, her eternal home, not too long after that on June 5, 2006. While I was understandably very sad at my mom's passing and I miss her greatly, as a believer the prevailing feeling is one of great joy, as she is now in Heaven. Her memorial service was wonderful, in no small part because she had planned it all out. It was as it should be and as she wanted it to be—a celebration. She had put all of her affairs in order, and we had an opportunity to enjoy each other and reminisce about her and the lessons that she taught us, through all those years around the dining room table.

Shortly thereafter, I began my second stint with CBS, this time as host of the NFL on CBS. Weekends are both enthralling and exhausting during the season. Because CBS Sports is located in New York, I travel every Friday to the city, usually by train. It requires less travel time than flying does all told, and I can more easily work reviewing the clippings and press releases for the week that may provide pertinent talking points for our show. Each NFL club will release its own set of press notes for that weekend's game, full of tidbits such as "the Colts are 6–1 when leading at halftime against teams located west of the Mississippi that are also north of Dallas" or something to that effect. They often are helpful by way of background preparation, though, so I do try to familiarize myself with all of those. Our football insider, Charley Casserly, the former general manager of the Washington Redskins and Houston Texans, usually travels with me. Shannon Sharpe has convinced me that the appropriate

Saturday morning activity—to add to the preparation for our Sunday show—is to work out with him, or more accurately, *try* to work out with him. Shannon retired from the NFL in 2003 as the all-time leading tight end in receiving yards, a record that stood until 2008. Shannon has, in recent years, decided to trade in his NFL-tight end type body for a body-building body; he has, in short, gone from merely really big to impressively chiseled. He is about six-feet, three-inches tall and two hundred forty pounds—all muscle. I, on the other hand am, well, not.

His workouts are grueling, making me use muscles which I previously doubted existed, at least in me. Worse yet, they take place at an incredibly rapid pace; he won't allow more than thirty seconds to recover between exercises. This past year I invited our CBS colleague, Jennifer Sabatelle, to join the Saturday workouts. Like Shannon, she's a workout fanatic, making my Saturday mornings doubly challenging.

I can live with that, but it's the fact that we then clean up and head over to an afternoon meeting at CBS, when every muscle starts to tighten up, that makes me rethink my commitment to Shannon and trying to keep pace with him once a week.

We arrive Saturday in the afternoon at the studios for our production meeting, conducted by our producer, Eric Mann. Eric is a longtime industry veteran who has won twelve Emmys, directed three *Super Bowl Today* shows, produced shows for two winter Olympics, and has produced the NCAA Men's Basketball Tournament studio show since 1991, and the NFL on CBS studio show since 1994.

Eric, a graduate of Northwestern, is as bright as he is tireless. And he is truly untiring.

We are seated in one of the only rooms I've seen at CBS that is of a size actually appropriate for its purpose. In the center of the room are two couches and three leather chairs. Those of us who are "on-air talent," Shannon, Dan Marino, Boomer Esiason, Bill Cowher, Charley Casserly, and myself, are seated in this area, along with Pat Kirwan. A former member of the personnel departments of the Buccaneers and the Jets, Pat provides research and behind the scenes support for our background research through his network of connections throughout the football world. In addition, seated in a row on one side of the room, are about ten others—writers and researchers—without whom our studio show could not occur. It is truly a team effort—each of the people in that room will be vitally necessary for the success of Sunday's broadcast.

We spend Saturday in an informal roundtable, discussing items that are certain to be in the broadcast the next day ("Can the Packers stay undefeated?" "Did the Packers make the right decision, letting Brett Favre go?") or Eric, standing at the head of the room, will throw out ideas, to see if there is sufficient interest, around which he and the writers can create a show segment ("Will any teams go winless this year?"). We will then debate those ideas in general but not get too specific. Eric doesn't want the actual live event on Sunday to lose its spontaneity—although it's difficult to imagine that happening in any room that contains Shannon Sharpe.

After a couple of hours, it is back to the hotel to continue to study for tomorrow's games and then to rest. It will be a long and exhausting Sunday.

Sunday begins with a wake-up call at five in the morning, and we are on the way to the studio by 7:30 a.m. Once we arrive we get dressed—my wife Dorothy is my wardrobe stylist having selected a season's worth of Troy McSwain suits—and go to makeup. It took Bill Cowher a little while to come to grips with makeup—you don't spend most of your life as a special teams player and defensive player, and as the head coach of a football team in a blue-collar city like Pittsburgh, and use makeup on a regular basis. Bill has transitioned nicely into the studio, however, although we all joke with him that it's only a matter of time until he goes back into coaching. We'll be sorry if and when he does.

Following makeup we get up to speed on any happenings of the morning—any late-breaking illnesses or injuries that we usually find out about through Pat and Charley and their network of coaches and front office members, and then we rehearse. I then call my wife to pray with me and for all of us for the day. I have learned not to go on the air without having prayed first.

Dan Marino and Boomer Esiason are the other two members of our weekly show. Both were very successful NFL quarterbacks, and there are occasional rumors that pop up that they don't get along, which they find amusing. They get along great. Boomer has thrown himself full bore into the media world, also co-hosting a very popular morning radio show on WFAN in New York each weekday morning, for four hours, and has used his platform to raise awareness and funds for cystic fibrosis and various other endeavors that help others.

Dan is still a hugely popular Hall of Famer, and a sought-after endorser. He is no less gracious with his time, though, and has also used his platform to help charities and others in need. I remember a New York Knicks basketball game that we were leaving at Madison Square Garden on a Saturday shortly after I began at CBS. We were in a hurry, trying to get back to our respective hotels to get a good night's rest, and darted out of a side door and across 31st Street into Boomer's SUV and we were pulling out of the parking space, when we began to hear voices calling after us. "Dan!" "Mr. Marino! Wait!" "Wait!" We turned and saw two guys in wheelchairs, racing across the sidewalk. Dan rolled his window down and urged the two young men to be careful, and we watched from the other side of 7th Avenue in horror as our pursuers wheeled their chairs in front of oncoming traffic. They crossed without collision—somehow—and came up to Dan. Dan spoke first.

"Easy there, guys. I don't want to see you getting hurt."

One of them gestured toward his chair. "What—and hurt us further?" Dan, Boomer, Shannon, and I still laugh about that, to this day. Dan signed the jerseys and footballs that they had. I have never seen him unwilling to go out of his way to interact with people; I admire that.

Finally, at noon, the lights come up on the set and we

begin speaking with our viewers, an audience which has been growing steadily over the last two years. We try to have fun as well as provide information and analysis as possible. Eric Mann views us as a hybrid between news and entertainment, so while we will always have fun and make the show lighthearted, we also begin our telecast with news of the day. Eric takes great pride in the fact that we will often give viewers substantive information on weather, injuries, and other late-breaking game developments at the outset of the show. At the same time, with Shannon in our midst, it will always be lighthearted for the viewers and the rest of us—whatever our role on the set.

That hour from noon until one consists mainly of us analyzing the upcoming games and sharing various bits of wisdom, like Shannon noting that the locker room at the old Veterans' Stadium was so small that "he had to go outside to change his mind."

Once the games kick off, Bill, Boomer, Dan, and Shannon take a break. I stay on the set, while Eric stays in the control room, still talking with me on my earpiece, along with the forty or so other people responsible for everything from tracking the progress of games to creating graphics for the screen to switching from one game to another to calculating the interplay between CBS Sports online and the television broadcast. I don't know how Eric does it all.

Every few minutes, at understandably random times, Wayne (our lead game-day statistician and researcher) or one of our other statisticians will call out through the set. "Touchdown, Indianapolis, Game Three. Reggie Wayne six-yard pass from Manning. Second quarter. Seven to seven." I will flip through my notepad to Game Three. All the games have been assigned numbers and the monitors on the set have those numbers posted as well. I will often ask if there were any key plays on the drive. The answer comes a moment later. "Yes, a fifty-six yard pass to Clark from Manning." Eric will then find times for Gamebreak, sending my voice into the homes of people watching a given game. He will tell me that we're showing the highlights of Game Three to the viewers of Game Six. I place my pencil on Game Six, so I call the announcers by their correct names, and then turn in my pad to my most recent notes on Game Three. They patch me into the broadcast, and I'm alone on the set, while my voice is live on the air.

"Hello to you, Gus and Steve and to all of you watching Arizona and Miami. Out in Nashville, Peyton Manning and the Colts knot the score at seven with the Titans on this six-yard touchdown pass to Reggie Wayne. The key play on that drive—a fifty-six yard completion to Dallas Clark. Now, back to the peripatetic Gus Johnson and his partner, Steve Tasker."

They keep the audio on the set long enough for me to hear Steve ask Gus—and the viewers—if I was saying something bad about Gus. Far from it, and they knew it. Gus had worked another event for CBS in Miami the night before the game. He likes to tease me about going to Harvard, and expects some big words now and then—I knew that somebody in the broadcast truck would be telling them in a moment that peripatetic meant "well-traveled." Sure enough, at the next game break, Gus leads in by saying, "Now let's go back to New York

and our own sesquipedalian JB for an update on Indianapolis and Tennessee. JB?" I thought his use of "long-winded"
was a nice comeback. Probably a better rejoinder than my
later reference to him as "indefatigable." I know that keeps
the day fun for us—and hopefully the viewers as well.

As we approach halftime, our statisticians distribute
highlight sheets that correspond to the highlight video
packages that they have assembled, and each of our guys
is assigned a couple of games. For instance, Boomer might
have Games Two and Four (Green Bay/Denver and Cleve-
land/Buffalo), and Bill has One and Five (Chicago/Miami
and San Diego/Oakland), and so on. We will all spend a few
minutes rehearsing, and then Eric sends those games that
have gone to halftime to us for updates from around the
league. This continues until the early games have finished,
around four o'clock each Sunday.

The networks have a strange way of counting viewers.
For the networks on any given Sunday, the one-hour pre-
game show generates ratings, which are measured and com-
pared against each other. However, if the early games end
early and there is any sort of studio lead-in segment before
the network begins broadcasting the late afternoon game,
the viewers for that late segment—even if it's only a minute or two—count toward the overall studio show ratings.
Because the viewers are always bigger for the late shows, that
increases the ratings. Following the "bridge show," between
the early games and late games, if any, we repeat the cycle of
cutting into games for updates, rehearsing, and performing
our halftime highlights, and then more updates. I usually

end up concluding the day's games by myself with a quick recap of scores. It is rare that we finish all of the late games and can do a full recap show with all of our guys before it's time to join *60 Minutes.*

As a team we have great chemistry. Since 2006, I'm told by Eric Mann and others that the ratings race has become extremely competitive and we've enjoyed several wins over that span of time, which had never occurred before—significant, in that it comes against what is a formidable FOX NFL Sunday team. All that we can do is to do our best by continuing to prepare diligently, stay focused, have fun, and play the roles we were meant to play.

I have always been introspective, but it seems like I'm taking even more opportunities to reflect these days—when Dorothy can get me to sit still, anyway. Maybe it's that I now have a granddaughter. I am so proud of my daughter Katrina who is married to a wonderful man and together they have blessed us with a precious granddaughter who I love doting over. Katrina has taken a break from school to be with Kaela, but assures me she'll be returning to finish. Education is so important to reaching those future dreams, and I believe she and her husband see that.

It has also allowed me to step back and look at some of the other things that I'm doing. I'm still involved with children, as I'm on the ministerial staff at my church and have been a part of the adult committee working with the youth ministry for the past nine years. The God's Covenant Youth Ministry meets once a month, and Dorothy ably and faithfully assists me with her regular attendance during my busy NFL season.

One of my other passions is the JB Awards. I was asked six years ago by Pat Allen, the former COO of the NFL Players Association, to lend my name and efforts to the annual NFLPA Gala, an event whose goal is to raise awareness of NFL players who are contributing to society and giving back—to reward their inherent desire and responsibility they understand in being role models. The stated criteria are to recognize players—each club nominates one—who demonstrate a "commitment to achieve excellence off the field through building better communities and stronger families." Communities and families. It doesn't get any closer to my heart than that. In addition to recognizing NFL players who have done this, we also raise money for the Special Olympics in DC, raising over a million dollars each year. I love helping out that wonderful organization, and to be able in the process to use my limited celebrity to raise up the example of guys who are bettering the world—it's a very special and humbling role I try my best to live.

Not everything I do is in a formal capacity. Like most of us, many of the things we do take place in the everyday moments of life. I simply need to remember to be intentional about it. To be aware of those moments all around me when someone needs to be reminded how special they are, when someone needs a moment and a lift up in life. An NFL owner called me not too long ago with an issue he needed to discuss. We chatted for a while, and I said that I was about to board a flight but would call him when I returned home that evening. I then received a second call, again chatted for a bit, and once again said that if it was all right, I was boarding a plane and would call him that evening—I had one call to place first and then I would call him back. My attorney, Jeff Fried, was with me and asked who the second caller was.

"The eighth-grade son of the receptionist at one of Brown Technology's business customers." Jeff looked puzzled, so I continued. "I met a receptionist over at one of our customers—I was waiting for a meeting to start, and we began talking. Go figure—me, meeting a new person! She was telling me that she was working hard to try and keep her son focused. He is a bright young man but she's worried about some of his friends, and wants him to continue to do well in school. I gave her my number and told her that I would love to speak with him. It's been two months—I had started to wonder if he ever would call."

In fact, that is a major reason that the technology company I co-founded with my business partners Reggie Brown and my brother Terence Brown, Brown Technology Group, even exists. We wanted to find a way to help—to hopefully create jobs for young people, and to teach those young people the Ingredients for Successful Living along the way. Jay Nussbaum from my days at Xerox was the catalyst in helping us to develop a strategic partnership with himself and a serial entrepreneur by the name of Bob LaRose. We are enjoying good growth as a company and young people will be a significant part of that continued growth.

I'm excited as well about being a minority owner of the Washington Nationals. The Lerner family was kind enough to gauge my interest in the club and then to ask me to buy into their ownership group. I do like baseball, although I can't attend very often with my schedule, but my main reason for investing was the opportunity to play a role in reviving interest in the game by minorities and to ensure that the financial pie associated with the ballclub would be more inclusive. In addition, it feels good to see myself, a local kid with a very modest DC upbringing, now having an ownership interest in one of the highest profile businesses in the city. Like my decision to attend Harvard, I'm hoping that this will serve as a positive example for others.

I hope kids see that there are significant opportunities for them to be as meaningfully involved in pursuit of their dreams as they'd like. That the dreams they have in their hearts were placed there by God and are to be pursued. That their dreams are not limited to sports or music only, which are worthy areas to succeed in for sure, but that this generation can also own a business, and touch lives all around them. And to think that it was merely two generations ago that my grandfather owned a Negro League Team.

Following the 2007 season, I went on a trip with Dorothy. I needed to get away—I was still grieving over the passing of my mother, and then a beautiful young girl by the name of Hunter Ozmer died. Hunter and her father Hunt had come up to Dorothy and me a couple of years earlier in a restaurant near our home and introduced themselves. They told me that Hunter suffered from Niemann-Pick Disease and that, although she was only sixteen years old at the time, she had already outlived most projections. I was thrilled to lend my name and assistance to increase awareness of this awful disease, but Hunter was the driving force. She really championed the cause, raising awareness as she fought the good fight. When she took a turn for the worse, Dorothy and I were able to use my business partner Bob LaRose's plane to fly to Roanoke to see her before she died, passing in early January, 2008.

So Dorothy insisted that we get away, and no sooner were we on our way before we ran into a bunch of kids in the airport who had matching T-shirts: "God Always Wins." I loved the sentiment and realized, the more I thought about it, that it's true in all areas of life. My mom died, leaving a void in my heart. I left FOX, not because I was looking to. I almost lost out in marrying the woman God had chosen for me, and I told a football television audience that a player was tackled on the sixty-yard line.

Time and time again, life hasn't gone according to plan. Time and again things happen—no matter how challenging, how painful, or how unexpected.

And yet, through it all, one thing remains:

God Always Wins.

EPILOGUE

It was April 7, 2008, and the Washington Nationals were playing the Florida Marlins at Nationals Park in DC. It was our home opener, and for once, I was early. I stepped off the crowded elevator into the club level, which was fairly warm—maybe from the throngs of people who had gathered for the beginning of the baseball season—despite the chill in the evening air outside.

Jeff Fried, my friend and attorney, waved at me from across the hallway. I waved back. I would be over by him in a moment so we could go into the Owner's Box together to watch the game. It was still an hour before game time, and the Nationals were still taking batting practice. I had plenty of time to get over there. Somebody tapped me on the arm and we began talking.

I arrived at Jeff's side, all of thirty feet from where I had stepped off the elevator, in the third inning. It had taken me just under ninety minutes to finally get to Jeff's side. He shook his head as I greeted him—he had seen this played out before.

I just love meeting new friends and interacting with old.

*   *   *

Two months later I was headed to another game—my second of the season—with Nathan Whitaker, my co-author. We had four tickets, so Don and Kris, two of Nathan's law school friends, were headed to the game with us. None of us had checked the weather.

I was driving down the George Washington Parkway when the drops of rain started to dot the windshield. As we traveled on we wondered how we thought that we were going to get a baseball game in—it was dark in every direction and now raining hard. We kept driving.

By the time we arrived at the stadium, the weather had cleared enough for them to start the game. We were, of course, late. But you knew that already.

We headed down to our seats just as the rain started again, so we decided to head up to the Lerners's box. The Lerners had invited us to come up to visit with them and their guests, so we took them up on it, rather than go to our seats and fight the elements. We visited for an hour or so, and then finally took our leave and decided to head home. I'm not sure if the game had resumed, but I am sure that I'm an early to bed sort of guy, and my time was fast approaching.

Kris commented that they—himself, Don, and Nathan— made up the "lamest posse" ever accompanying a celebrity. I responded that I was quite all right with that. It felt like the four of us had known each other for years. As we headed back, the rain started falling heavier than before, and frogs—big, giant frogs—began jumping across the parkway, presumably from the Potomac River some forty yards away.

Epilogue

"Frogs are bad enough, but if locusts come next, I'm outta here," said Don. We all cracked up, and thankfully, there were no more plagues that visited us that night.

After they dropped me off, Nathan tells me that they took him aside. "Is he always like that?" Nathan wasn't sure what they meant.

"He spent more time talking with the woman running the elevator at the stadium than he did with Chief Justice Roberts or Michael Milken." That was true. It was a pleasure meeting those gentlemen, but the box was crowded and others wanted to make their acquaintance (like Nathan, who looked as though he might have forgotten his name when he was introduced to the Chief Justice of the United States), so I took the opportunity to meet some other people there as well.

Then, as we were leaving, I asked the woman running the elevator her name and where she was from. As it would happen, Joyce had grown up in DC and attended Anacostia High School. I knew that school well. We had spoken for a while, and then on the way out—as it had been on the way in—there were a number of people that we passed that I needed to stop and speak with. New friends.

"He's always like that," Nathan told them. He told them about our trip to New York in which I knew each of the hotel staff by name—the bellhops, the front desk clerks, the housekeepers. It still seems natural to me. Why shouldn't we get to know each other and learn about each other's families?

Frankly, I'm not sure I see the big deal. I only share that about my mind-set so that—in case you don't realize it already—

you might realize that there is a whole world out there that would love to meet you and interact with you. People with the same needs, fears and joys, who just may have gone to high school down the street from you.

As for me, there's no question that I'll keep meeting those people. It's how I was raised, to understand that people are fascinating and special. And, it's part of the role that is mine to play—to learn about people and hopefully encourage them and lift them up a little bit higher, to shine a spotlight on them, and how special they are, for all the world to see.

It's how I saw my mom and dad treat people. It's how in the last few years of my mom's life, when she was house-bound and spent most of her time in bed, she conducted or performed her ministry of helping people. When *she* was the one battling the ravages of diabetes, she was encouraging others, strengthening *them*. When in the hospital the final five months of her life, hospital workers and the like found themselves coming by her room to meet this woman who met every medical challenge with a peace and confidence that only God gave her. She didn't focus on *her* issues, but lifted others up, standing firmly on *His* Word every day. She had me read Bible verses to her every day I visited her in the hospital. They strengthened her. So, it's not difficult or a problem for me to encourage others, to get to know them, because it's a role that we all can play, for a lifetime.

NOTES

Chapter 6: The Foundation Determines the Height

1. But, speaking the truth in love, may grow up in all things into Him who is the head—Christ—from whom the whole body, joined and knit together by what every joint supplies, according to the effective working by which every part does its share, causes growth of the body for the edifying of itself in love (Ephesians 4:15b–16 NKJV).

2. Other translations use different terminology, but I believe the point is the same. The New International Version refers to being "prosperous and successful," while the New Living Translation says that "you will prosper and succeed." Both contemplate something additional to "success."

ABOUT THE AUTHORS

JAMES BROWN, a native Washingtonian, graduated with a degree in American government from Harvard in 1973 where he was a three-time All Ivy League basketball player. JB is a three-time Emmy winner as Outstanding Studio Host. He is currently the host of CBS Sports' *The NFL Today* and Showtime's *Inside the NFL* and formerly the co-host of *FOX NFL Sunday*. He is co-founder of Brown Technology Group, founding partner of the Washington Nationals, and an ordained minister. He and his wife Dorothy reside in suburban Washington, DC. His daughter Katrina is married to John Walker and they have a daughter, Kaela.

Nathan Whitaker is the co-author of three *New York Times* bestsellers, including *Quiet Strength*, which reached number one and is one of the bestselling sports-related titles in history. A two-sport athlete at Duke University, Nathan also holds post-graduate degrees from Harvard Law School and the University of Florida. He lives with his wife and two daughters in Florida.